They Were Giants in Those Days
Stories from the Heart of the Cariboo

They Were Giants in Those Days
Stories from the Heart of the Cariboo

Eldon Lee

Heritage House

Copyright © 1999 Eldon Lee

CANADIAN CATALOGUING IN PUBLICATION DATA

Lee, Eldon, 1923-
They were giants in those days

Includes index.
ISBN 1-895811-97-X

1. Cariboo Region (B.C.)—Biography.
2. Frontier and pioneer life—British Columbia—Cariboo Region.
3. Pioneers—British Columbia—Cariboo Region—Biography.
I. Title.

FC3845.C3Z48 1999   971.1'7503'0922   C99-911213-9
F1089.C3L43 1999

First edition 1999

Heritage House wishes to acknowledge the financial support of the Government of Canada through the Book Publishing Industry Development Program (BPIDP), the British Columbia Arts Council, and the British Columbia Archives and Records Service (BCARS).

Cover design by Darlene Nickull
Book design by Cara Patik and Darlene Nickull
Edited by Cara Patik and Audrey McClellan
Maps by Darlene Nickull
HERITAGE HOUSE PUBLISHING COMPANY LTD.
Unit #108 - 17655 66 A Ave., Surrey, BC V3S 2A7

Printed in Canada

Canada

It is only fitting that out of respect
to the Giants of my youth, that I
express myself in both their languages,
Chinook and English.

*Nixka [Nesika] Kopa tum tum
nika tikegh okoke papeh
mamook skookum wawa pe
wawa delate kopa hiyu
kumtux.*

It is my heartfelt wish that this
book carry a powerful and clear
message with much wisdom.

Eldon Lee, 1999.

CONTENTS

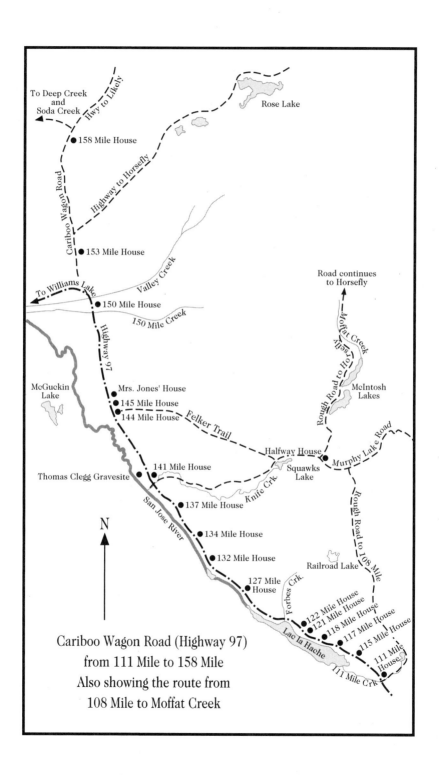

To Deep Creek and Soda Creek

Hwy to Likely

Rose Lake

● 158 Mile House

Cariboo Wagon Road

Highway to Horsefly

● 153 Mile House

To Williams Lake

Valley Creek

Road continues to Horsefly

● 150 Mile House

150 Mile Creek

Highway 97

Moffat Creek

Rough Road to Horsefly

McGuckin Lake

Mrs. Jones' House
● 145 Mile House
● 144 Mile House

Felker Trail

McIntosh Lakes

Halfway House

Squawks Lake

Murphy Lake Road

● 141 Mile House

Thomas Clegg Gravesite

Knife Crk.

San Jose River

● 137 Mile House

N

● 134 Mile House

Rough Road to 108 Mile

● 132 Mile House

Railroad Lake

127 Mile House

Forbes Crk.

122 Mile House
121 Mile House
118 Mile House
117 Mile House
115 Mile House
111 Mile House

Lac la Hache

111 Mile Crk.

Cariboo Wagon Road (Highway 97)
from 111 Mile to 158 Mile
Also showing the route from
108 Mile to Moffat Creek

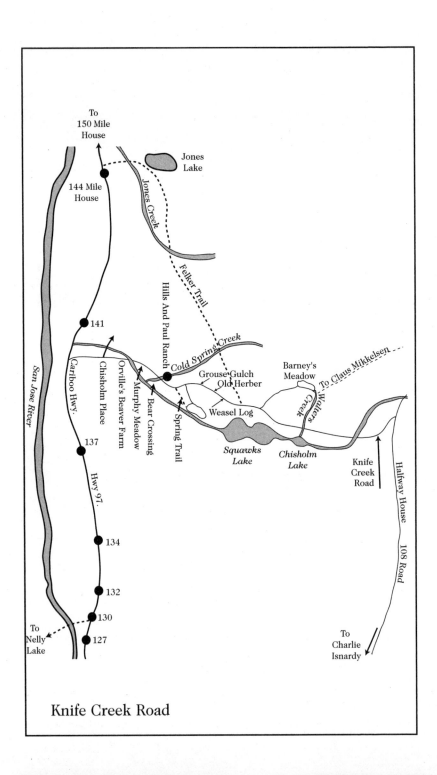

Knife Creek Road

FOREWORD

There are some places on earth that manage to transcend the simple boundaries of geography. Blessed with distinct natural beauty and the pride and passion of its residents, such a place adopts a distinct persona and grows its own identity. Add a history of unique incidents and a boundless arena for pioneer spirit to flourish, and such a place becomes a breeding ground for titans.

Such a place is Eldon Lee's homeland—the Cariboo. As a boy, Eldon's Cariboo was centred along Knife Creek Road. It started as a simple easterly trail that met the original Cariboo Wagon Road at 141 Mile House, an establishment closely tied to the gold rush in the 1860s.

Velocity has much to do with perspective. When travelling by saddle horse, horse-drawn wagon, or sleigh, trees, rocks, gulches, hills, and even logs become significant way-points, acquiring a relevance similar to that of the cities passed by today's high-speed traveller. Thus it is that Knife Creek Road attains a historical prominence out of proportion to its size.

The present Knife Creek Road bears little resemblance to the original. Although still unpaved, it is now a twenty-foot-wide gravel way, with culverts and drainage ditches, that joins the main road at the foot of 140 Mile Hill. The old Knife Creek Road, which originated on the southern bank of Knife Creek at the 141 Mile House, and this revamped road both had their moments of romance, mystery, and the occasional scandalous event, each an epic in local history.

To an extent, this book is inspired by James Michener's *Centennial*, a tome Eldon read many years ago. Michener conjured up a fictitious community in the American West and built a historical portrait that encapsulated the evolution of

North America's West. The real people, places, and events that occurred along Knife Creek Road over the past 150 years are no less symbolic of the evolution of the West and Canada as a whole.

The title of this book comes from a monument that is nowhere to be found today, like so many markers of history that succumb to time while the stories of people and events live on through the written word. In 1925 the Honourable Denis Murphy, a 55-year-old lawyer who served as an MLA in Victoria's provincial legislature and sat on the B.C. Supreme Court, was asked to help commemorate the building of the original road to Barkerville and the Cariboo gold rush. An innkeeper's son, Denis had grown up at 141 Mile House and was a first-hand observer of much that went on along both the main Cariboo Wagon Road and its dusty tributary, Knife Creek Road. At the unveiling of the monument, Murphy extolled the virtues of the Cariboo people in an impressive speech that called upon his oratorical skills and classical training. As he ended his tribute to the pioneer men and women, he read six simple words inscribed on the cairn that he had unveiled: *They were giants in those days.*

INTRODUCTION

I grew up surrounded by the oral tradition of the Shuswap people and was aware of the impact it had on storytelling in the Cariboo. That was the way of life along Knife Creek Road. The elders knew things that no one else knew, elders like Old Annie Basil.

The wise people of the Shuswap and other First Nations can remember the distinct subtleties of their different myths and their versions of nature and the beginning of time. Collectively they have become a single story of creation in my mind, one that represents the early learning of my youth. I want to tell that story the way it was told to me, and make *wawa*, talk, to say how it was in times long ago.

In the beginning there was only the Great Spirit, and the Great Spirit was everywhere. This was a long time ago, more moons than any Indian could count. The white man got it all wrong. They said that everything started with a big bang and a round little ball. Indians know better: everything started with a big splash and a big lake with a muddy bottom.

Two muskrats digging in the mud at the bottom of Squawks Lake made that big splash. First they dug up a big mound and made all the land; then they formed little mounds and made the mountains; then they dragged their tails in the mud to make the Fraser River and Knife Creek. The Great Spirit told them to go down to the bottom of the lake again and bring up the trees and all the plants, and then bring up all the animals and the fish and the birds and the whales. The whales went out to sea, and he sent the salmon up the river to make little salmon and then they were sent back to the sea.

Squawks Lake, where it all began.

When this was all done, the Great Spirit patted the little muskrats on their backs and told them that they had done well but that there was still something to be done, something too sacred for the muskrats to do. Only the Great Spirit was wise enough to make this creation.

The Great Spirit made a big fire and blew on it, and the sparks flew up to make the stars and the sun and the moon, and then everything was light like the sunshine and he took a handful of mud and squeezed it in his hands. From one side of his hand came a strong Indian brave and from the other side came a pretty little Indian maid, and since there was nobody else they looked at each other and decided to make a wigwam together. So the big chief took the woman, and soon there were little babies coming every year, coming in the middle of the summer after every long winter.

The chief would go out and get fish and find deer and moose along Knife Creek, and the pretty squaw made the fire and cooked the meat and fish, the babies came, and she made coats and moccasins for everybody. At that time everyone was happy. The muskrats were happy, the fish were happy, the moose and deer were happy, and the big chief and squaw and all the little babies were happy.

After a time, a bird came along that was smarter than all the rest, a big black bird, the raven. This bird would lie

*and steal and cause trouble. One day he came and called
the Indians together and asked them if they were happy, and
all the people said they were, and so the raven said to the
people: "You're happy, but you could be more happy if you
had more and if you didn't have to work so hard to get food.
Make bigger nets and catch more salmon and more fish and
make fish pens and kill more bear and deer and moose."*

*The people did this, and soon one fish pen was too close
to another, and the Indians started to fight over the best
places to fish and they killed many deer and moose.*

*At that time the mountain goats were special friends of
the people and came down from their mountains to play with
the little Indian boys and girls. The mountain goats were not
wild at all, and one day the people said, "Why should we
walk all over to hunt when we have the goats so close to
us?" So the Indians started killing the mountain goats. One
goat had a beautiful baby goat, and the young people chased
after it and killed both of them. All the mountain goats ran
away and went up to the top of the McIntosh Mountains,
and there the Great Spirit talked with them and they told
the Great Spirit how wicked the people had been and how
wasteful.*

*The Great Spirit told them to build a long house and invite
the Indian braves and chiefs to a great feast. While all the
chiefs and warriors were seated and eating huge mounds of
food, the mountain goats would pull the long house down
and everyone inside would be killed. The mountain goats
thanked the Great Spirit and did exactly that.*

*Since that time the goats have lived on the peaks of great
mountains to the east, and the Indians must hunt very hard
to find goats or deer or moose.*

*At this time the Great Spirit saw how the Indian people
wasted the salmon coming up the stream, and so he pushed
rocks across the Fraser River so the salmon could not go up
the river, and the Indians went hungry and starved and had
to hunt far and wide for food.*

*The people quarrelled and fought with each other and
forgot the Great Spirit, and the raven was always spreading
mischief and causing trouble. From that time on there were*

arguments and quarrels and wars and sickness and hunger and cold and storms and great wind. The Great Spirit and the people spoke to each other from a long way off, and things were never like they were when there was that big splash and the two muskrats and the shallow lake.

CHAPTER 1

THE BRIDGE BETWEEN THEN AND NOW

Old Annie Basil of Sugar Cane

We who came later little appreciated the ancient immigrants to the Cariboo. Ten thousand years ago, a time stretching back to the reaches of prehistory, nomadic people from Asia crossed a land bridge and migrated south in waves. These were Stone Age people without agriculture, who existed as a hunting and fishing society.

They blended into nature like a current in a stream, leaving hardly a mark on the land. They were like a garment warming the sleeping earth. Generations passed by and little changed until the white explorers came from the east. With trade and gold, the even tenor of the land was swept away in a wave of new and strange activity. Old Annie Basil was a bridge between two lifestyles, ancient solitude and modern frenzy.

As far as the old-timers could tell, she had been on the land forever. The image of her stooping to tend her potato patch seems as old as time itself.

She had been married to a man from the Shuswap village of Sugar Cane. She bore a number of children, who for the most part lived about her at Sugar Cane, although some had died. Basil is not a Sugar Cane name. According to some, the name comes from the Lillooet country to the south, and Annie may have been native to that area.

The Salish tribe to which she belonged extended from Alexandria, north on the Fraser River, southward to the

Columbia River. At one time there were two villages west of the Fraser River. They disappeared, likely from the ravages of smallpox and raids from the Athabascan tribe to the west. Over the past hundred years the interior branch of the Salish nation occupied lands east of the Fraser River.

Salishan is a difficult language, and I know of no white person able to speak it fluently, probably because of the use of clicks, clacks, grunts, and coughs for syllables. Annie herself never used Salish when talking to the whites, but only Chinook words. Apparently this was common practice. A tribal dialect tended to be exclusive to a given village, and outsiders were addressed only in Chinook or English. (Settlers of the central Cariboo were eager to learn the Indian language and were taught words supposedly in the Salish dialect. Later they learned that not one word belonged to the Salish speech. All of the words were Chinook.)

"I was a little girl, *nika klootchman tenas*," she said, "when the white man came. They spread like the green kinnikinik all over the country. Now you can't throw a stick without hitting two or three of them." And she laughed a thin cackle at her wit.

On her ancient feet she wore moccasins made from moosehide, serviceable except when rain came. If they got soaked, she ignored any discomfort. Activity kept the hide supple as they dried and also stopped them from shrinking. Her normal attire included a warm skirt, blouse, one or two sweaters, and cotton stockings suspended upward by some sort of fixation, the nature of which was unclear. Perhaps garters. Her extra clothing was washed in a creek at intervals and hung to a tent rope or pine tree to dry out in the wind and sunshine.

She was a skinny, lively little lady who, old as she was, still managed to lead her pack horse 28 miles from Sugar Cane on Williams Lake to the Hills and Paul Ranch on the Knife Creek Road. On these trips each summer, she pitched her tent 100 feet outside the corral fence and picketed her old horse with a 30-foot rope, one end attached to a tree and the other end to the horse's foot. This arrangement necessitated moving the animal twice each day to a new grazing spot.

Annie Basil, who knew everything
about the country that surrounded her.

Annie could live off the land. She said that she knew everything about the country that surrounded her. "I know this stick, that stick, this rock, that rock. I know every tree," she would say, spreading her arms around her to take in the whole environs. Early every summer she found wild strawberries before anyone else. She picked blueberries, raspberries, and huckleberries and shared the fruits of her labours with the ranch kitchen. She snared grouse with a looped buckskin string attached to the end of a fifteen-foot pole, and with the same pole landed ten-inch trout in Coldspring Creek.

It was fascinating to watch her capture a grouse. Taking up a position at the base of the tree on which the grouse perched, she raised the pole, keeping it well away from the bird and moving the loop of the buckskin from side to side. As she brought the noose towards it, the grouse seemed hypnotized, moving its head back and forth to watch the string. With a quick thrust, Annie would snare the surprised grouse, and dinner was secured amid a flutter of wings and a shower of feathers.

A VANISHING LANGUAGE: CHINOOK

Chinook is a language far removed from French, but it was the second language of the Cariboo up until 1950. Most people are familiar with words such as *tyee*, *cultus*, *skookum*, *mukamuk*, *wawa*. Few realize that these words are the last remnants of a language that once extended from Oregon to Alaska and from Vancouver Island to Alberta.

The famous Robert Service up at Dawson City, Yukon, wrote a book of poems entitled "Ballads of a Cheechaco." The last word, *cheechaco*, meant "newcomer" in Chinook.

During the first half of the twentieth century, many old-timers could speak Chinook and many courts had a Chinook interpreter on staff. British Columbia, with seven strikingly different native languages and then the languages of the big tribes—English, Chinese, and French—each unintelligible to the others, had a major communication problem. Chinook bridged the gap. What could be more sensible than one language that could be understood by all?

The Chinook language goes back hundreds of years and did not begin with the Hudson's Bay Company in 1860 as some think. There is evidence that it existed at least 200 years before white settlers came. There has always been trade between the Indian tribes, with commerce in salmon, oolichan grease, slaves, and handicraft products. A means of communication was necessary since tribal languages were distinct and exclusive.

In the eighteenth century the Chinook tribes along the Columbia River were active in trade, so numerous words are from the Chinooks. The next most common source is from the Nootkas on Vancouver Island and from the Salish tribes of Williams Lake south to Washington. The Tsimshians along the northwest coast also contributed a number of words. With the coming of whites, English and French words were simply added in to accommodate these strangers.

An advantage to Chinook is that once you learn a hundred words, communication is possible. In all there are about 2000 words, with no sounds difficult to voice. The language is simple, with many words having multiple functions. For example, *kopa* means with, by, to, towards, on. Those who favour gender neutral language will feel at home in Chinook—there is no gender. There are no articles (i.e., the, a, an). Present, past, and future time are indicated by adding a defining word to the verbs. Thus, *Alta nika klatawa* is "I go now"; *Ankutie nika klatawa* means "I went"; *Alka nika klatawa* means "I will go." There are no changes for number: *ickt mowitch* is one deer while *klone mowitch* are three deer.

A further virtue of Chinook is that it can be written in the Roman alphabet and read. Indeed, there was an Oregon newspaper, *The Oregon Native Son*, printed in Chinook.

Enough of *cultus wawa* (idle chatter). Here is an example of Chinook. Because of familiarity I have chosen a portion of the Lord's Prayer. "Nesika (our) papa (Father) klaksta (who) mitlite (dwells) kopa (in) saghalie (heaven). Kloshe (good) kopa (in) nesika (our) tumtum (hearts) mika (be your) nem (name). Nesika (we) hiyu (greatly) tickegh (desire) chako (to come) mika (your) illahie (kingdom)."

It was perfectly normal for the Salish residents of Sugar Cane to use Chinook words when speaking to us. I remember my grandfather, Arch Herber, talking to Liza Dick on the death of an old neighbour. "He was a *kloshe* man, he go to a *kloshe* place."

Liza replied tartly, "*Cultus man klatawa cultus illahie*," which meant that she didn't think much of his chance in the hereafter.

What is responsible for the passing of Chinook? I think it is one more black mark against television. The young watch television two or three hours a day, and English is the language that is used outside the village. It has pretty well supplanted tribal language as well. I know of only one man, now 80 years old, who speaks Chinook. Did I say one man? I meant one man besides the author.

Mahsie shicks klahowya (thank you friends).

She found other wild foods, like onions, Indian potatoes (a tuberous bulb found beneath carrot-like plants), and fiddleheads, a fern-like plant growing in swampy land. In the spring, sweet sap from young pine and birch trees provided sugar and could be distilled into syrup.

Stories along Knife Creek Road often included Annie and her contributions to the settlers' lives. She was midwife for Ellen Murphy of the 141 Mile House and delivered Denis, the supreme court judge of British Columbia who would commemorate Annie and others at the Cariboo Road monument. Old Annie always told us that she saved his life. At any rate, Denis obviously believed her because he sent her ten dollars every Christmas for many years.

Midwifery was a serious business in the Cariboo. Prior to 1940, giving birth could very well mean death for the mother. For every 140 babies born, a woman died during labour. One has to be amazed at the courage of women who looked forward to children. Indeed, the future of the whole land depended on having strong and healthy offspring, but it was a hard and dangerous process. For these women there was no decrease

Midwives like Annie Basil were often essential, especially if anything went wrong. Children were numerous in the Cariboo, and a family of twelve was not unusual.

in toil during their pregnancy, and they entered each labour with sure knowledge that they had to deliver that baby or die. There was no Caesarean section for obstructed labours, no air evacuation to major hospitals if they ran into problems. They lay on their beds in rude log cabins, bit down on a roll of cloth, and laboured for hours and sometimes days with no pain relief. If things went wrong, a midwife like Annie Basil would have been essential.

It seems that Annie didn't just save the lives of the newborn, but of grown men as well. Once, while camping at Squawks Lake, she heard cries for help and ventured out in the dark, wind-driven woods to locate and rescue a desperate and frightened party of *cheechakos* (newcomers). She was later told that they were important men in the government.

These memories go back to a time that history would label the Great Depression, when we were boys living at the Hills and Paul Ranch and Annie Basil was there. Next we were young men and she was old, almost 100, and she was still there. Now we are getting old ourselves, and old Annie Basil is gone. Her old horse is gone too. Her potato patch by a small pond near 150 Mile House is overgrown with weeds. Only the rocks on the hills are there. Maybe that's all that ever stays.

I hope old Annie Basil is in a better place now, some place like the Cariboo that she loved so dearly—but maybe there isn't a better place. If so, she is lucky to lie where she does, in the Cariboo.

CHAPTER 2

FAMINE TO FEAST

The Murphys of 141 Mile House

In the twentieth century, the old Cariboo roadhouses erected during the gold-rush era have added romance to the land. These homesteads acted as mile markers and were the centre of every imaginable happening: prosperity and ruin, intrigue and hard work, life and murder, and above all, adventure. This romance is gradually being lost to the depredations of time and the passing away of the pioneers.

The 141 Mile House shared in all of this, as its history goes back to the early 1860s. Some say habitation of the area began as early as the 1840s, and this is not as improbable as it may seem. The Hudson's Bay Brigade Trail of 1842, from Kamloops to Alexandra, passed close by, if not through, the original deeded land of the Murphys.

Old Annie Basil told my mother in the 1930s that the white man first came to the Cariboo when she was a girl. This would probably have been in the 1840s or early 1850s. What is known for sure is that Dennis and Ellen Murphy established the Deep Creek Ranch in 1862. This was later known as Murphy's, Murphy's Bar, Enterprise Ranch, and finally, after World War I, as 141 Mile House after the milepost of the Cariboo Wagon Road.

The Murphy brothers, Dennis and William, were from County Cork in southern Ireland, and like many of their compatriots they left Ireland for the New World from the port of Cork. They had just survived the great Irish potato famine. Almost a third of the Irish population had died of starvation. At that time rough cottages were scattered over the green, stony landscape, each holding its pitiful burden of emaciated bodies—father, mother, children, grandchildren—lying in rude heaps for want of nourishment. It is likely that for the Murphys, death had lost its shock value. Almost no Irish person in southern Ireland escaped hunger in those days.

It was with this mindset that Dennis Murphy and his brother arrived in the eastern United States, stayed for a time in New York, and then made their way to California. They travelled north to British Columbia in 1858, arriving at Yale in a dugout, and by degrees continued on up to the Cariboo gold fields.

Dennis Murphy, with the Irish love of land, needed little persuasion to give up the mining venture and settle into the fertile land of the Cariboo. He took his first land grant at Williams Lake and almost immediately abandoned it for a Crown land grant five miles up Knife Creek from the Cariboo Wagon Road. This was where Knife Creek Road had its formal beginnings. Natural wild meadows lay on either side of Knife

The Hudson's Bay Brigade Trail of 1842 may have passed through the original deeded land of the Murphys.

Creek, yielding hundreds of tons of wild hay each year. Shortly afterwards, a second Crown grant at the junction of Knife Creek and San Jose River gave Murphy acreage for a home ranch 400 feet lower than the hay meadows. This second acquisition had a more temperate climate, and Knife Creek Road connected the two land holdings.

The need for more hay to feed hundreds of cattle drove the road further to the east, eventually linking it to the 108 Mile Road in 1866. The latter road ran from 108 Mile House to Horsefly River and had served as an alternate route to the major gold fields.

Dennis and
Ellen Murphy.

The Murphys combined a ranching venture with a stopping house for travellers on the road. During the next few years a substantial log house was built, as well as a barn capable of holding 24 horses, which was erected across the road. The upland was cleared of rocks and brush, opening up about 200 acres. This provided sufficient hay for a substantial herd of cattle and horses during the winter months.

The Barkerville newspaper of the time wrote that "old Dennis Murphy can be seen ploughing his fields with teams of oxen yoked to sod-turning farm equipment." The same newspaper told also of the delicious meals and luxurious

*St. Joseph's Mission school, near Williams Lake, provided
education for the Murphys and other Cariboo children.*

sleeping accommodations to be found at the 141 Mile lodging.
A typical dinner consisted of baked ham, beef stew, potatoes,
fresh beans, carrots, fresh-baked bread, ranch butter, three
different pies—apple, saskatoon berry, and custard—two
puddings, and tea.

A cow barn was constructed across the road from the main
house, and the milking of eight to twelve cows provided a
supply of dairy products. Denis Murphy, the son of Dennis and
future B.C. supreme court judge, later proclaimed that his
hands were the strongest of any judge as a result of milking
cows on his family's 141 Mile House ranch.

In the Cariboo, upland hay requires extra water beyond
normal rainfall, so the Murphys needed an irrigation system if
they were to survive. With considerable engineering skill they
dug a ditch, starting at the three-mile mark of Knife Creek
and connected to what became known locally as the Chisholm
place. It was at this level that Dennis Murphy's elaborate
irrigation system began. It is fair to say that the Murphys were
somewhat careless with the blasting materials. Live explosive
primers could still be found in the rocks a century later. A
small dam redirected water into this irrigation system, which
traversed the hillside, crossed the Cariboo Wagon Road via a
log culvert, and then channelled down to the drinking pond
beside the horse barn. The pond provided water for the stock
year-round and doubled as a winter skating rink for the Murphy
children.

A tributary ditch parallelled the wagon road and served to irrigate hay land sloping towards the west. A half-acre garden supplied potatoes, cabbage, carrots, strawberries, raspberries, and currants, which flourished in the red soil at the 2300-foot elevation. Wild saskatoon berries and chokecherries grew in profusion in the creek bed.

For 90 years the 141 Mile House served as both the Murphys' home and a recognized roadhouse providing accommodation, dining facilities, and a pub. With the wagon road only 60 feet away and an inviting white picket fence, many a weary soul sought shelter there.

It is difficult to see how passers-by could have been accommodated when the Murphys themselves had six children. Paying guests shared three log buildings between the main house and the bank of Knife Creek. Also built in this space along the bank of Knife Creek were an icehouse, machine shop, and outdoor privy.

The ranches along the Cariboo Wagon Road often suffered from inadequate supplies of hay in their immediate vicinity. The 141 Mile House was no exception, so Dennis Murphy

*Johnny and Margaret Murphy in
front of 141 Mile House in 1890.*

pushed eastward along Knife Creek to ensure adequate hay to feed his 600 head of cattle. The big "Murphy Meadow," five miles up Knife Creek, acquired in 1862, provided much-needed bottomland on both sides of the stream. The ranch must have seemed a daunting affair to the Murphys and a far cry from the ten-acre plots of their native Ireland.

Murphy, a feisty man even on his best days, found occasion for a lawsuit over a settler's grant eight miles to the east. Dennis Murphy finally acquired title in 1892, and the meadow is known to this day as "Disputed Meadow." Another story tells of testy old Dennis Murphy making his way determinedly down the road, wagon wheels rolling steadily in the two defined ruts of the road. All was well until a neighbouring rancher approached, plodding in the opposite direction, his wheels moving in the same ruts. The horses came nose to nose and the oncomer suggested politely that Dennis move to the right (vehicles in B.C. drove on the left until 1910). Dennis replied, "Ruts? You like ruts? These are my ruts. Go find your own."

The early Cariboo ranchers faced relentless odds as they struggled to become self-sufficient. The milk cows provided dairy products and the chickens laid eggs. The surplus egg supply was preserved in waterglass solution in large porcelain crocks. Swine at butchering time gave fresh pork, and hams and bacon were cured in a log smokehouse, enough to supply the needs of the ranch over the year.

Fresh beef or pork was a problem since refrigeration was only available in the cooler confines of an icehouse. There meat was hung in screened enclosures to keep flies at bay. Even so, meat rarely kept for more than ten days. It was common practice for one ranch to butcher an animal and share the meat with adjoining ranches before the summer's heat and flies led to spoilage.

Dennis and Ellen Murphy occupied the ranch for the next half century. Over time they acquired title to extensive ranch holdings of 2500 acres. A puzzle is presented by Ellen, a staunch Roman Catholic, who had only six children. One can be sure that the Murpheys in Ireland regularly exceeded this family size, and in consequence, the population of southern Ireland had boomed, leading to the Irish famine of 1845. Interestingly enough, it was the potato that was responsible for the large families in Ireland. The lowly potato was a good source of nutrition and vitamins and could be cultivated almost anywhere in Ireland. With this source of food, couples married at a younger age and families were larger.

The 141 Mile House, at 2300 feet, did not have the bountiful potato crops of Ireland, but the nutrition generated seemed to yield proud results. The six Murphy children all reached adulthood. They started their schooling at St. Joseph's Mission school, six miles from the ranch. The Murphys had helped establish the school and worked to instil high scholastic standards before their children moved on to universities in the east. In this pre-railroad era, distance alone restricted travel back and forth, so the children were separated from their parents and the ranch for years at a time. Denis recalls spending the three months of summer vacation in Quebec, where he learned French.

In the end, all the children benefited from good education. One became a lawyer, another a supreme court judge, and Johnny continued to manage the ranch. Mystery surrounds the fate of the youngest son, Thomas Francis, born in 1876. He acted as a sponsor for Johnny Murphy on a land deal in 1913, but is not mentioned in other family chronicles. The M-backward-J brand of the ranch became famous throughout the Cariboo. The brand was first registered in the 1880s, and it was still recognized 80 years later.

During its heyday, the 141 Mile House was the source of much speculation. Stories and rumours still persist of various shenanigans that occurred there. Gambling and fights have been alluded to, and several people have alleged that murders occurred. Emma Young, wife of the stagecoach freighter Al Young, was born at the 144 Mile House. A near neighbour for twenty years, Emma portrays the Murphys of 141 as a wild bunch, fighting and arguing frequently at the pub. That they were a quarrelsome, pushy clan, quick to take offence and slow to give up a grudge, is still part of Cariboo folklore. Mrs. Young once told my mother about a traveller who was murdered at the bar during a violent argument and in the night was stuffed into an abandoned well at the back of the Murphy house. The well was reputedly filled in, and subsequently a small log shed was constructed over the site. Looking at old pictures of the 141 Mile House, which is now destroyed, just such a structure can be seen behind the house and slightly up the hill. Certainly old Dennis, who had survived the horrors of the starvation of so many in Ireland, wouldn't have been shocked by one more stiff.

Adding fuel to this persistent rumour was the discovery of a potential murder weapon. Racehorse Johnson (see chapter 18), a later owner of the 141 Mile, found a hidden revolver when he replaced a portion of the living room floor in the 1920s. One chamber had been fired.

In spite of such stories, the Murphys enjoyed a substantial presence in the Cariboo district. Devout Roman Catholics, they were instrumental in establishing St. Joseph's Mission. Always active in their support of the church, they helped argue the legal battles over land titles in the area of the Mission Ranch. The suit was lost, but old Dennis, with the light of battle in his eyes, pressed the church to appeal the decision. The church declined, with an eye to its public image.

After he took over the 141 Mile House in 1896, Johnny Murphy was instrumental in establishing the Enterprise Cattle Company, a consortium of nearby ranches with similar business goals. Unfortunately, this dream faded with his death in 1918.

The Murphys by and large did not make old bones. Most died before age 60. The original Dennis and Ellen Murphy and their sons Johnny and James lie in St Joseph's Mission cemetery. William, their oldest son, an oblate priest, is buried in Hull, Quebec. A fire around 1960 destroyed the old house built in the 1860s, but the ranch that was established so long ago continues to be active. Perhaps this gives foundation to the old Irish belief that the land is all that matters, that the land alone endures.

CHAPTER 3

A PARTY OF PLEASURE

Dr. Cheadle and Lord Milton, the First Tourists

There is no doubt that British Columbia's Cariboo District enticed a fascinating blend of humanity to its frontier. Possibly inspired by David Livingstone's first grand journey up Africa's Zambesi River (1853-56), a new generation of British Empire adventurers descended on the Canadian West in the 1860s. Among this band of remittance men, missionaries, old soldiers, and young adventurers was a young doctor named Cheadle and his companion, Lord Milton.

These two scions of privileged English society, Dr. Walter Cheadle and Viscount William Fitzwilliam Milton, left their comfortable homes, their high tea with triangular cucumber sandwiches, and their strawberry crumpets with clotted Devon cream, anxious to respond to the challenge of a new country. They were young and high-spirited, aged 28 and 24 years respectively. Dr. Cheadle was large, six feet tall, and sturdily built. Lord Milton was shorter by several inches, plump, and red-faced. They had decided to cross Canada, visit the gold fields, advance the commercial interests of Britain, and establish new trading routes to Asia. These ambitious objectives were only for show. They really took the trip out of a craving for adventure, freely admitting that it was "a party of pleasure."

They left Liverpool in early June, and while Cheadle coped with the North Atlantic, Lord Milton soon became seasick.

Landing at Quebec City on June 30, 1862, they proceeded to Montreal, then Toronto, and finally into the United States where the Civil War was brewing. They headed westward to re-enter British territory north of Minneapolis en route to Fort Garry. From Fort Garry the intrepid tourists journeyed to northern Manitoba, to a small settlement called Belle Prairie. There they lived with the Metis and Natives, shooting a number of the great lumbering buffalo. From the buffalo they took choice cuts of meat, the tongue, and marrowbones. These were necessary provisions for the winter that they would spend in a small log cabin. To be sure, this must have been a crowded living arrangement in comparison to their stately homes in England.

In mid-April of 1863 the adventurers left their winter quarters and pushed on westward, riding saddle horses and leading two pack horses. A Metis guide and his wife travelled with them to Jasper House. They followed the North Thompson southwest to Kamloops, enduring fearful hardships along the way. They arrived half-starved, gaunt and tattered, having killed two of their horses for food. Their journals record both daily routine and more shocking discoveries. At the top of the list was the sight of a headless Indian sitting by his North Thompson campfire.

From Kamloops they travelled to the coast, and even though the Fraser Canyon road was not yet open, they set out by steamboat and went upriver to Douglas, north across Harrison Lake, from there by mule to Anderson Lake, then walked the last few miles to Lillooet. From Lillooet they took a stagecoach along a dangerous route over Pavilion Mountain to Clinton. Here they were able to join Gustavus Wright's new road, and the next day they arrived at 100 Mile House.

In their journal they described the Cariboo countryside as rolling and pleasant, dotted with farms growing short-stemmed barley, wheat, and vegetables. The cattle looked well-fed and well-bred. But more than the beauty of the Cariboo, they were fascinated by the morbid happenings of the area, and Cheadle pinpointed the murder site of a clerk of the Lillooet freighting enterprise E.T. Dodge & Company. Young Tom Clegg was apparently shot in the head less than a quarter of a mile from the nearest house ahead. That house was 141 Mile House, and the site of the murder was at the foot of 140 Mile Hill.

Anxious to get to their Barkerville destination before winter set in, they did not seek the hospitality of old Dennis Murphy of 141 Mile. This may have been wise on their part. The cantankerous Irish Catholic hated the English and may well have been murderous in his attitude.

The express stage travelled twenty to forty miles a day and rocked fearfully as passengers bundled up against the cold October weather. Smothered under coats and damp blankets, the stage occupants smelled rank at best. Still Cheadle and Milton could not complain; they smelled also, so they took up space in the coach and ate their share of the limited food supplied by the roadhouses.

From Soda Creek, a steam-powered paddleboat called the *Enterprise* carried them 60 miles to Quesnelle Mouth. The captain, J.W. Doane, treated them hospitably, loaning the two Englishmen his personal cabin and toasting them with champagne every fifteen minutes. They thought him a jolly fellow, but were glad to get off his ship.

A sketch from Dr. Cheadle's journal depicts
the living conditions of early roadhouses.

Excerpts from Dr. Cheadle's Journals

Travelling North - October

Steamer came in about 2 o'clock bringing a host of miners two of whom were very drunk and continued to imbibe every five minutes; during the time we stayed in the house they must have had 20 drinks. The swearing was something fearful. After we had been on board a short time, the Captain finding out who we were, gave us the use of his cabin, a comfortable little room and supplied us with cigars and a decanter of cocktail, also books and papers. We were fetched out every few minutes to have a drink with someone, the Captain (Doane) taking the lead, by standing champagne all round. We had some dozen to do before supper; no one the least affected, Milton and I shirking in quantity. The Cap told us the boat was built on the river all the timbers sawn by hand, her shaft in five pieces packed up on mules, cylinders in tow, boiler plants brought in the same manner. Boat cost $75,000.

Travelling South - November

Cocktails every five minutes, and champagne lunch afterwards. Happiest man I ever saw. Steward tells me he takes a cocktail every ten minutes while on board. Very jolly fellow. Had to give a keg of brandy to his men before they would haul the steamer on to shore. Gave them a champagne dinner on being paid off today, and we heard them singing away below deck. Came in for many champagne drinks during the day.

Since the vessel was out of service for the winter, Cheadle and Milton journeyed from Quesnel to Soda Creek in an open boat that had Forty passengers ... crowded into it, packed close as Negroes in a slaver.

The Enterprise *carried champagne, a jolly captain, and many adventurers to Quesnelle Mouth.*

A 50-mile walk took them to Barkerville, where they made full use of their brief visit to crawl down mine shafts and collect a few nuggets of gold. The return trip from Barkerville to Quesnelle Mouth took place in a foot of snow at the beginning of November. Uncomfortable lodging, poorly prepared meals, and a second journey on the *Enterprise* brought little pleasure.

It was not until they reached Frank Way's Deep Creek House opposite the 164 Mile Post that their fortunes improved. From there they proceeded to Davidson's at 150 Mile, where they settled in for the better part of a week. They entered into the true joys of touristing, enjoying reasonable beds and excellent meals featuring milk, cream and butter from the dairy, and a good selection of vegetables from the garden. Dr. Cheadle walked the three miles to the head of Williams Lake for a hunting foray, only to bag two partridges.

Exhaustion and weariness had slowed the draft teams. When the stage to Clinton arrived, Milton and Cheadle passed the 141 Mile House without comment and arrived in the dark at the Blue Tent Ranch, where a large blue-and-white tent had been erected the previous year by Henry Felker while he built a roadhouse. The next morning, after an early embarkation, the pair enjoyed breakfast at Anderson's Lac la Hache House, ten miles further south.

As they made their way through the treacherous Fraser Canyon, thoughts of home began to preoccupy the two adventurers. Once in Victoria they booked steam passage to California and rail service to Washington, D.C. When they arrived, the U.S. capital was in turmoil due to the fierce and bloody Civil War battles carrying on in near proximity.

On March 7, 1864, 21 months after setting out from Liverpool, Dr. Cheadle and Lord Milton arrived home to some acclaim. They were both made fellows of the Geographical Society and soon published *The Northwest Passage by Land*. It was an instant success.

Lord Milton, never in good health, died at the comparatively young age of 39 years. Dr. Cheadle became a famous medical practitioner and took a professor's chair in Charing Cross Hospital in London. He received some criticism because he was a firm champion of women's rights in medicine. However, in the end he prevailed. At age 75, full of years and with much recognition, he passed away, known as one of the Cariboo's first tourists.

150 Mile House in 1900. Dr. Cheadle and Lord Milton stayed here for a week as the first tourists to the area.

CHAPTER 4

THE GOLDEN FLEECE

How the Lees Came to Knife Creek Road

Jason and his comrades were the first Argonauts. These original adventurers in early Greek legends ventured to far lands, avoiding grave dangers like the Clashing Islands and fiery bulls. They confronted challenge and temptation in their quest to retrieve the golden fleece.

The argonauts of Knife Creek, my forefathers and their fathers and mothers, travelled a parallel course to that of the ancient Greeks. They left behind familiar, secure homelands in Europe, braved the menacing Atlantic Ocean storms in tiny ships, and then challenged a giant land, only to emerge themselves as giants.

I trace these argonauts back to a woman named Betty Hague, who arrived in North America in 1620. This would be small potatoes to Old Annie Basil, whose ancestors arrived 10,000 years before, probably walking across a land bridge from Siberia to Alaska. Betty, on the other hand, arose from her hotel bed in Portsmouth, England, walked two blocks, and boarded a flat 80-foot ship destined for America. Her name was not even recorded on the ship's manifest, because only male heads of family were listed. Generations later, one of her female offspring would marry into the McLane clan.

Allan McLane, with six kin in the front ranks of the Battle of Culloden Moor, felt it wise to leave Scotland in 1746. Decades later he was a loyal colonel for the revolutionary army (he tipped General George Washington that Benedict Arnold was a traitor). For his service he was made port captain of Baltimore after the war. His picture still hangs in the Library of Congress.

Perhaps there was an ember of 1746 smouldering in the McLane line that led Charles McLane to forego a thriving business in California and, with his widowed mother Sarah Jane, journey to Prince George, B.C. In the growing community there, he established another business. In 1928 he heard word of the dissolution of John Murphy's Enterprise Cattle Company. McLane had a choice of two ranches. The first was the 134 Mile House on the Cariboo Road; the second, the Hills and Paul Ranch eight miles up Knife Creek Road. He opted for the beauty of the Hills and Paul and purchased this 1000-acre ranch for $3000, including a $1000 mortgage that was to plague him for the next twenty years.

He failed to consider that eight miles of Knife Creek Road would lie under snow for six months of the year. Thus it came about that Charles McLane had a ranch and no means of operating it. His solution was to recruit his relative Archie Herber from California.

The Hills and Paul Ranch, mile eight, which had seen many owners, but none like the argonauts.

At the far end of Murphy's Meadow at Mile 6, the road forks toward Powers Meadow, then past old Murphy's Disputed Meadow, and finally arrives at a small ranch on Knife Creek. The other branch continues on as Knife Creek Road, then approaches the land of my youth. The road goes down across a spring, between open fields to the right and pine forests to the left, and finally along an upland meadow of clover and timothy hay. This is the Hills and Paul Ranch of 100 years ago. Scattered about the meadow, a dozen large piles of rock give testimony to back-breaking toil, when bushel-sized stones were piled onto a low sledge and pulled by team to each collection area. These stones were originally deposited courtesy of some meandering glacier, which dropped sediment collected many miles to the north.

The Hills and Paul Ranch, set halfway between the Fraser River to the west and Timothy Mountain to the east, was pre-empted in 1902 by John McIntosh of Halfway House on nearby 108 Mile Road. He had occupied the land several years earlier, but without formal ownership. Newspapers on the walls of the

The argonauts (left to right): Margaret Barclay, Larry Barclay (California friends), Howard (holding son David) and Alice Lindstrom, Archie, Ethelyn. Back row: Barney, Stanley, Shirley, Eldon, Todd, Pat, and husband Melvin Mayfield.

Archie and Ethelyn Herber in 1946, long after settling their home in the Cariboo.

original building carried dispatches from the Boer War in South Africa. Successive owners were Hills and his partner Paul, Johnny Murphy, Enterprise Cattle Company, Charles McLane, the Lees and Herbers from California, then Don and Ruby Gray from Oregon. The current owner is Clifford Hinche, a native son.

It was suggested to Archie that he travel to the Cariboo and view this ranch before committing his family to anything monstrous, but Archie was determined to undertake farming in the Cariboo. In May 1929 he sold his California holdings (I remember ferrying a load of squealing pigs across the Sacramento River to their new owner), then loaded all the family's worldly possessions into a 1925 two-ton Ford truck and a 1928 open Ford touring car. At 10 a.m. on May 20 we headed for Canada, and in so doing became worthy of those intrepid ancestors who had come to North America. The argonauts were nine in number: paterfamilias Archie Herber; materfamilias Ethelyn Herber; Alice, age 19; Wayne, 18; Stanley, 12; Patricia, 10; and Shirley, married, with two children, myself barely 6 years and Carrall (Todd), 4. My father, a somewhat wild and irresponsible second-generation Californian, refused to go and was left behind. My mother, who had spent two winters in Canada keeping her Uncle Charlie and Grandmother Sarah company ten years before, may have had some misgivings, but approached the challenge with a spirit of adventure.

During the first day of travel we covered less than 40 miles of the 1500-mile journey. A brand-new rear tire had to be replaced, and we spent the night in a campground near Sacramento. The next day we realized that the four tons of impedimenta on the two-ton truck was an impossible load, particularly with the mountains of northern California to come. The piano was shipped by train, and a ton of household articles was left with friends at Redding. The California hills proved a challenge, and everyone had to get out and push the truck. The car was enlisted as well and pulled with a stout rope attached to the truck.

On the twentieth day, Charles McLane and a new vehicle met us and led the way onto Knife Creek Road. The steep inclines and curving carry-ons were behind us. Still, the final eight miles proved to be daunting. The cars became stuck in a mud bog after a mile, and the truck had to be temporarily abandoned. At 10 p.m., June 10, 1929, while the last traces of dusk were still on the horizon, we arrived at the Cariboo ranch that would be our home for the next 21 years.

Although 1000 acres in size, the ranch had insufficient hay supply (100 tons) to support enough livestock to provide a living. The two-storey log house had five bedrooms, no indoor plumbing, water from nearby Coldspring Creek, and light from coal-oil lamps and mantles of gas lamps. Worst of all, at an altitude of 2300 feet, it was not possible to grow corn, tomatoes, or fruit because of early frost. In some summers, the potato plants froze in early August.

While the women unpacked and made the house into a home, the men repaired the farm machinery and acquired Beauty, a roan milking cow. Uncle Charlie found a team and wagon in Prince George, and Archie, towing a mower, covered the 200 miles to the ranch from Prince George in ten days. Somehow we rallied to face the first winter.

It was unlike anything ever experienced by our family. With two feet of snow, 40-below weather, and prolonged isolation, it was nothing like California. For the first time in our lives we heard the ear-splitting crack of aspens in the intense cold.

In addition, we argonauts did not feel completely comfortable with Canadians. They were excessively polite, always saying "thank you" or "excuse me," and mangling words such as "roof," "either," "neither," "down," and "town." They also seemed to have some adolescent attachment to royalty, such as Lords, Counts, Dukes, Kings, and Queens, that had all been disposed of by Americans for 150 years.

Gradually, we settled in. Thank-you's and excuse-me's became more common in our speech, we found that the Canadians became more charitable in regard to their pronunciation of "roof" and "either," and their attitude to royalty seemed less pronounced.

The argonauts had certain characteristics. There was a love of knowledge and a desire for learning. Debate and reference to dictionaries and resource books interrupted dinners. Thousands of books of every sort were avidly read. The result was that three of us from the Hills and Paul Ranch went on to advanced degrees. Stanley returned to California after ten years, received a scholarship in chemistry at the University of California, then changed to theology for a bachelor of divinity (B.D.) at Asbury. Todd took sociology in the States and went on to a B.D. at the University of British Columbia. I became a medical consultant after thirteen years of study.

Self-reliance was seen as a virtue, and the family did not rely on the government or anyone else for that matter. We felt that the best government was the one least likely to complicate our lives. There was a mutual dependence among members of family, an unwritten rule that if one was an hour overdue for a rendezvous or a return home, someone would be out searching. This rule generated a sense of responsibility and punctuality that remains to this day.

Hospitality was assumed. No one came to the ranch without an invitation extended to share in a meal, and at evening a visitor was invariably invited to spend the night. Passers-by who were thought to have lice were directed to sleep in the hayloft in the barn.

A philosophy that dictated that good fences make good farmers must have made our views seem somewhat racist by today's standards. We did not breed our short-horned cows to

Holstein bulls, and did not see a virtue in the mixing of the races. There was friendliness and respect accorded to people of other ethnic strains, and they were regarded as equal, but not the same. It would have been unthinkable for a marriage to be contracted with a person of another race; even a Russian or French person was off limits. However, we could always truthfully say, "Grandfather Henry Herber died in the Battle of Gettysburg in 1864 to liberate all people of every race and

*The Cariboo house that the argonauts reached
in 1929. Pat Herber is in the vehicle.*

colour." Not too many families could make that claim. The Herbers had been pacifists and could have easily avoided the Civil War by claiming that it wasn't their fight. However, they hated injustice more.

From my youth I can readily recall the abundance of foods that graced our home. At breakfast, mugs of steaming coffee or tea accompanied hot biscuits dripping with butter and spread with preserves or fresh pickings from the raspberry, strawberry, or blueberry patches. This was followed by oatmeal porridge sprinkled with brown sugar and covered in clotted cream. Other hearty foods included home-cured sausages rich with the savour of sage and pepper, white gravy from the drippings, hashbrown potatoes, eggs fresh from the chicken run, and perhaps eggnog or custard at the end. Dinner was a special event and was even more substantial. A blessing over the food, heads bowed, always preceded the meal. A hearty soup came first, followed by stewed chicken, noodles, mashed potatoes, carrots and peas, fresh baked Parker-house rolls, and for dessert, chocolate cake with bowls of fruit or custard. At bedtime, hot chocolate and a second piece of cake encouraged sweet dreams and sound sleep.

Women strongly influenced the spiritual life of the family. Children were instructed in biblical verses, and eventide vespers were led by the mother. There was reading of scripture, and everybody knelt for a prayer, with favourable mention made of leaders, deserving or not, ministers of the Lord, missionaries, family members, and for special concerns of daily life. Often prayer was given for neighbouring ranch families. Prayer and bible reading were a natural aspect of our lives. Evening prayers were lengthy, sincere, and usually answered. Sunday was a day of rest. There was a natural rhythm to life, and resting on the seventh day was part of that rhythm. On Sunday morning with family, workers, and friends, a morning service was held with readings from scripture and devotional materials. Tithing was strictly practised; that is, one tenth of income was given to the Lord's work. I recall that once, after a period of limited income, $1400 was received in a lump sum. Of this, a tenth, or $140 was given to the church, much to the surprise of the church minister. It was no surprise that from the ranches along the eight miles of Knife Creek Road, four ministers of the Lord came forward. Rules of temperance were strongly adhered to and no alcohol was permitted in the home. There was a song that we used to sing:

> I'm a temperance advocate,
> can't you see
> And those big brewery wagons
> ain't going to run over me.

A brewer may hand down the queen from her carriage, but the devil himself would have been more welcome in the argonauts' home. Smoking was also not allowed on the ranch. There was a poem that my Aunt Alice was fond of quoting:

> Tobacco is a filthy weed
> It is the devil's own sown seed
> It drains the pockets,
> Scents the clothes
> And makes a chimney
> Out of the nose.

The author and Todd Lee, with their mother
Shirley outside the Murphy's 141 Mile House.

There is always the temptation to seek wealth and leisure, to find the easy way. The original argonauts have gone on, and their grandchildren are coming into the front lines. Now it is the task of this generation to change the world, to make right the wrongs, to make straight the ways. I can only hope that they, like the argonauts of old, always challenge the frontiers and confront the unknown.

CHAPTER 5

DREAMS AND GHOSTS

The Felkers of 144 Mile House

They were a diverse lot who settled the Cariboo land, put down roots, and endured. The Felkers from Hanover, Germany, arrived in North America in 1848 and made their way across the United States to the gold rush in California. The trail of gold ran from California northward, and they eventually settled at the 127 Mile House on the Cariboo Wagon Road. In 1862 the family consisted of Henry George Felker, his mother Mary, his wife Antonette, and four children— George, John, Johanna, and Henry, all born as the family made their way across the United States. Henry was a rolling stone. Louisa, the fifth child, was born at 127 Mile House; William at Walla Walla, Washington, as the family travelled by wagon back to Montana; and Emma, the last, was born at the 144 Mile House upon their return to B.C. Emma liked to claim that she was a confederation baby, coming into the world in 1867, but modern archives put her birthday in 1869. When she was 60 years old, Emma came to 142 Mile House to live with her daughter Dora Labonty. Emma had a sharp tongue and bright white hair. I recall receiving a severe scolding for shooting her granddaughter with wheat stuffed into an air gun.

Emma was educated at St. Joseph's Mission and remained on the 144 Ranch until she was 21, when she married Joe Bellmond, a miner at Quesnelle Forks. Two children were born there—Dora Antonette and William Francis. Subsequently,

Antonette and Henry George Felker,
of the sturdy Cariboo type.

Emma left her husband and the miner's life that she hated and managed the Palace Hotel in Clinton with her children. There she met Al Young, a dashing teamster of the Cariboo Road, and took him as a second husband. This too was not a "till death do us part" relationship. With time she booted Al out.

The ranches situated along the Cariboo Wagon Road were dependent on upland hay to feed their livestock, and the Felker Ranch at the 144 Mile House was no exception. Because of the uncertain supply, they were forced to go eastward to wild meadows at Jones Lake, Lot 38, three miles away, and then to a second meadow, Lot 39, on Jones Creek a mile onward. Antonette Felker then pre-empted a further meadow, seven miles east on Jones Creek, called to this day the Big Felker Meadow. Hay from these holdings had been harvested for years before formal title was obtained. This was a common practice in those days.

The Felkers built a wagon road from the home ranch to Jones Lake in 1866, and this was extended to Big Felker Meadow and to Squawks Lake and Chisholm Meadow on upper Knife Creek Road. The road, known as the Felker Trail, gave easy access to wild hay meadows at Halfway House and the Lazure Meadows at McIntosh Lake.

This trail was popular with miners anxious to escape the miseries of 108 Mile Road. From Halfway House, many went west on Knife Creek Road, turning onto the Felker Trail at Squawks Lake. In a mere ten hours they reached the 150 Mile House, where the fleshpots, hotels, and bars of civilization were at hand.

The Felkers held considerable animosity towards the Murphys. This was the result of the proximity of the two ranches where water, cattle-grazing rights, and land were a matter of contention. As well, Louisa and husband Tony Ulrich were involved in a legal battle with old Dennis over a meadow on Knife Creek Road. The meadow is called Disputed Meadow to this day as a fallout from this 1888 quarrel.

Of the seven original Felker children, the oldest, George Henry, born in 1849 in St. Louis, ended up owning the 144 Mile Ranch. On his death in 1923, he left the ranch to his four children—George Jr., William Richard, Elsie Antonette, and Cecilia May Violet (George, Dick, Netty, and Violet). His nephew Harry, a son of John Deddrick, was manager of the

William Philip Felker who died of cancer
soon after marrying his wife, Fanny.

ranch, but none of the children could live with Harry and left. When, after fifteen years, the ranch was returned to them by the terms of the will, it was so deeply in debt that it had to be sold. Orville Fletcher purchased it in 1948. After 80 years, the Felkers' ranch was under a new owner.

The Felkers are gone, but their spirits remain. William and his mother were thought to haunt the old 144 buildings. And I believe that to aid modern adventurers, Henry Sr. still freshens his original blazes as he treads the paths and portions of wagon road that remain from the old Felker Trail.

The ghosts of the Felkers are said to still roam their beloved Cariboo.

CHAPTER 6

THE MUSTANG'S CHALLENGE

Harry Wright of Nelly's Lake

William Wright came to 127 Mile House, then called the Blue Tent Ranch, in 1867. His offspring continued there for over a century. His son John raised his family at the ranch, and four of John's sons settled along the Cariboo Wagon Road. Bert had the ranch at Lac La Hache, Harry at 130 Mile House, Ernie the 132 Mile Ranch, and Clem the 137 Mile.

Clem at the 137 Mile had bad luck. Both he and his wife died at comparatively young ages of cancer, their daughter Catherine died of breast cancer, and their son Douglas died of multiple sclerosis.

Ernie at the 132 Mile lived in an idyllic dwelling, a white two-storey house situated on a curve of the old Cariboo Highway and close to the San Jose River, where a heart attack claimed him. His wife Enid lived into her nineties and passed away in 1997 in the seniors' residence at 100 Mile House. Ernie's large hay meadow, Big Swamp, lay close to the Disputed Meadow of the Hills and Paul Ranch.

It was Harry Wright that we knew best. He was a good neighbour, albeit ten miles away, and a good rancher. In the fall he could be seen miles away from home, moving a half dozen cattle ahead of him. In early winter, half covered with snow, he rounded up cattle for transfer to his feedlot. He seemed impervious to the weather and was reluctant to stop even for a cup of hot tea brewed over a campfire.

*One of the few
likenesses of
Harry Wright.*

Harry was known for his horses. He was the number one horse wrangler of the central Cariboo, a dedicated pursuer of unclaimed mustangs. During the first half of the century, bands of these wild horses roamed the wilderness west of the Cariboo Wagon Road in an area centred around Nelly's Lake. After 1919, with the completion of the PGE Railway, this was referred to as "across the tracks." It was a very rough terrain, strewn with rocks and covered with pine, aspen, and willow trees. Game trails led to scattered meadows growing swamp grass and to small potholes dotting the countryside. Five miles southwest of the 130 Mile House was Nelly's Lake. This was a shallow, clay-bottomed lake with a swamp meadow along the southern tip. A rocky shoreline bordered the remainder of the lake, and a 50-metre grassy boundary lay between the lake and the aspen trees beyond.

It was there that the bands of wild horses roamed in complete freedom. These were descendants of horses brought to Mexico centuries before by the Spaniards. There were usually six to ten horses in each band, which was headed by a stallion. A number of mares, either pregnant or about to be, were jealously guarded, and other males were driven away with furious violence. Several yearlings or colts were usually included in the band, and once in a while an elderly gelding was tolerated. His role was to keep watch on the colts, and he took no interest in the mares. In this he was akin to a eunuch in a Far Eastern royal household.

In the summer, the horses' main activity was grazing, and they wandered from one grassy area to another, congregating in thicker bushes at midday to protect themselves from insects.

In winter, they would gather in low-lying areas where swamp grass maintained its nourishment under the snow, which provided the only water from November to April. Healthy horses survived the most severe winters. If a horse entered the winter season old or sick, a fall would be fatal, and predators were everywhere. As a point of interest, horses do not often lie down in the winter. They sleep standing up, with legs locked and eyes closed, motionless. A thick coat of hair stands on end and provides good insulation from the cold.

At one time in the 1930s, the horses had multiplied to the point where it was deemed desirable to thin their numbers. A bounty of five dollars was put up for each horse killed. The reasoning behind this was shaky at best. The idea was that killing the horses freed up the range for cattle, even though the country across the tracks was unsuitable for that purpose. Many horses were needlessly shot and their ears delivered to the government agent for the bounty.

Some people have golf for a hobby, some hunting, some fishing. Harry Wright's hobby was chasing wild horses. Each fall after the hay was stacked, he rode across the San Jose River at Wright Station and headed for Nelly's Lake. It was the Wild West all over again when a band of horses was found. Harry would yell, spurring his little bay mare over the ground in hot pursuit of the mustangs. His horse was grain-fed, providing endurance that wild horses, fed only on grass, could not match. The mustangs would be winded after only twenty minutes, their lathered sides heaving.

Lady and her foal, Silk Stockings, both rescued from a hard life in the wild by Harry Wright.

The stallion always challenged the cowboy, head high, ears laid back, but it was only for show. He knew his harem was lost, but Harry was generous in victory, separating out any worthwhile stock and herding them back to 130 Mile House. The stallion and remaining females were allowed to go free. Harry loved the adventure of the chase, and the five dollars received for each animal recovered was like free money. He was a worthy and honourable opponent, and we sometimes wondered if the horses loved the chase as well and missed him when he retired to Albion in the lower mainland in 1950, selling the 130 Mile House Ranch and leaving the Cariboo.

CHAPTER 7

JOKERS AND JUSTICE

John Haley of 130 Mile House

When we arrived in the Cariboo from California in 1929, the first person we met was John Haley. He filled the position of manager, overseer, worker, and general factotum of the Hills and Paul Ranch, eight miles east of the 141 Mile House. A laid-back individual at 50, he took us in and gave us some indoctrination into a strange land.

"Yes, the winters do last six months," he told us. "No, the mosquitoes do not carry malaria, but they carry everything else, including horses, cows, moose, and humans."

We, who were used to California summers with heat and dry, desert-like weather, could not get used to rain in the summer. When we asked whether it always rained, John answered laconically, "No it doesn't always rain in the summer—sometimes it snows."

We came to appreciate this soft-spoken, middle-aged ranchman with brown, drooping moustache, greying straight hair, and twinkling blue eyes. He dressed more like a farmer than a rancher, with woollen work pants, plaid shirt, and ordinary work boots.

We found that he had gained his experience the hard way. For a number of years he had been a stump rancher, first on a small holding south of Quesnel, and more recently on his ranch four miles east of the 130 Mile House, halfway between Knife Creek Road and the Cariboo Highway. A wandering, rocky wagon road through the forest connected the Knife Creek Road and Walker Road with his small 160-acre holding.

His ranch was a cleared open space in the woods. In the centre of this was his twenty-foot log cabin. A lake surrounded by rushes occupied the eastern limit of his holding. This lake supplied ducks and geese for his larder, and in wintertime, muskrat pelts supplemented the income from his beef sales. For many years these holdings were referred to as Haley's cabin, Haley's meadow, and Haley's lake.

John lived alone, but there was a persistent rumour that this had not always been so. While living in North Dakota, rumours of an improper relationship between his wife and his neighbour became too much for Haley to bear. Infidelity was a crime akin to claim jumping or cow rustling, serious offences in the Old West. Culprits often ended up hooked on a rope

John Haley and friend, c.1930, at the Hills and Paul Ranch.

looped over a tree branch. Haley, being in a charitable mood that day, simply filled the offending neighbour with lead from his six-shooter. Fearing a miscarriage of justice from city lawmen, he departed for the Cariboo.

There was another John Haley story, retold year after year. He was not a great housekeeper, but the hospitality code of the Cariboo dictated that any hungry traveller was invited to a meal. To one such guest, John served up the usual moosemeat stew along with minimal conversation. When his companion got to the bottom of the plate, he noticed that it was nailed to the table.

"Damn it, John, what is going on here?"

John Haley exploded. "If you can't accept a little progress, you can get the hell off my ranch and stay off."

He had little education and few diversions except hard work, bad weather, and difficult memories. Still John maintained a certain optimism and zest for life. Each spring he planned some new enterprise, like enlarging his meadow, building new fences, or irrigating more ground for hay. Nothing could have convinced him that his ranch would never support him. Nor could he accept the fact that his only means of survival lay in taking small jobs with the neighbouring ranches. With the onset of the Great Depression, these jobs became scarce because money was so tight.

As is common with those whose means of livelihood is marginal, John Haley's health deteriorated. His ever-present rolled cigarettes led to cancer of the throat. Extensive surgery cleared the disease, but left him with a swallowing deficiency and the inability to smoke. Addicted to nicotine, he found a means to inhale by closing his nose with two fingers. The cancer finally got John for good at age 65, and he died in Kamloops. He remains to this day an example of the spirit of perseverance despite hardship, the sort of spirit that was responsible for the making of the Cariboo.

CHAPTER 8

COWBOY TO CATTLE RANCHER

The Dream of Harry Barnard

At marker 2225 on the forestry access road from 150 Mile House to McIntosh Lake is a swamp meadow. On the right, a narrow road leads to a crumbling log cabin and barn with its roof fallen in. This is all that remains of a dream.

Harry Barnard, known as Barney, was the last of a vanishing breed. He was a cowman who still caught the mystique of the Old West, and ranching and cattle were in his blood. In 1935, aged 40, Barney arrived in the Cariboo sporting a Stetson hat, worn but polished boots, open shirt, stylish jacket, and whipcord pants. He was plump, but he sat on his horse like he was made for his saddle. Tip, his bay horse, was short-eared, plug-headed, and when fully alert, looked half-asleep. However, he was one of the best cow horses in the Cariboo.

Barney's ambition was to make that quantum leap from cowboy to cattle rancher. He had saved $2300 from his salary as a hospital orderly in a Washington hospital and reckoned this sufficient to get him started as a rancher. He leased a meadow and built a cabin and barn. He bought 100 cows, two teams of horses, harnesses, haying equipment, wagon, and bobsleigh. Instantly, he was a cattle rancher and accepted by others as one of their own.

The first winter came, and with it, evidence of weakness in his plans. His cattle were on the soft grass on the Knife Creek range. An early cold spell in November put them on the feedlot to survive on swamp hay for the next six months. Many, including Barney, believed that cattle would thrive on swamp hay. This not being the case, he lost 20 percent of his herd the first winter.

While his cattle grew thin on their feed, Barney grew fatter. He was an excellent cook, and his homemade doughnuts, cheddar cheese, and chocolate were a powerful magnet for my brother and me. At every opportunity we sent our saddle horses racing across the seven miles to his one-room log cabin, where he filled us to the brim with crispy cake doughnuts and steaming mugs of hot chocolate.

Life in these isolated situations is hard. The constant cold, the loneliness, silence, and monotony get to the strongest people. Many individuals cannot survive even a few days of this before cabin fever sets in. A situation commonly encountered in B.C. during the long winter months, cabin fever is more recently referred to as "S.A.D. Syndrome" (seasonal affective disorder). After my time as a doctor, I became familiar with the signs of cabin fever. Loneliness and anxiety would develop into withdrawal and depression, then avoidance of any human contact, and finally outright psychosis would strike. Barney was able to resist cabin fever only by spending a day every week with us at our ranch, where fellowship and friendship were available.

Barney, with a moose that he killed.

His sociable nature sometimes got him into trouble. One day a neighbour came by with a bottle of rum. Barney, in a thoughtless moment, took a swig, completely forgetting the strong temperance bent at the Hills and Paul Ranch. No one was allowed entrance to our ranch home if they smelled of liquor. Barney had to spend hours outside on the porch until the noxious fumes were expunged from his breath.

Another aspect of Barney's character was a loyalty to the ideals of the Old West. Cattlemen solved their own differences. One day he found one of his cows bawling at the fence of Jake L., a neighbour. Inside Jake's pasture was a calf with a fresh brand, and Barney believed that the calf belonged to his forlorn cow. When Jake refused to part with the calf, Barney said nothing. Later that fall, Barney turned up with wonderful moosemeat. In fact, I could have sworn it was beef!

Cabin fever was endemic in isolated cabins such as this.

The Cariboo is dotted with isolated log cabins, and Barney's holdings saw the same fate. He endured for a few years and then sold everything to Harry Felker of 134 Mile House. His meadow lies abandoned, and his cabin and barn are falling apart.

It wasn't cabin fever that got to Barney. It was the dream of being a cattle rancher that was his fever, and it burned him up and finally sputtered into ash. When he died, I wonder if the natural inhabitants of the Cariboo didn't acknowledge his defeat somehow. Perhaps a lone coyote sounded a farewell and night birds a last requiem.

CHAPTER 9

BRANDY OF THE LAMBS

Auntie Gertie of Knife Creek Road

T he spirit of Gertrude Tressierra still moves over the flat of land where Knife Creek, tumbling between willow-lined banks, makes a sudden turn southward before resuming its westerly flow. She had roots in the Cariboo going back hundreds of years, and there is rich history associated with her maiden name, Dussault. The original settler, Eli Desceau, born in 1610, came to Quebec from the French village Montaine-la-Calvan Ifte Veille in 1630 and, according to Gertie's great-granddaughter Donna Sweet, was a Protestant, likely a Huguenot of the Calvinist persuasion. Six generations later, her father, Joseph, now a Quebecois Roman Catholic with the family name spelled Dussault, came west from the village of St. Antoine to the gold fields of British Columbia.

Her parents' relationship had romantic beginnings. Joseph, travelling with a group of miners, became ill and was left at Soda Creek at the Sellar's farm. After weeks of convalescence he improved, but his

Auntie Gertie.

comrades had gone on to the gold fields. By that time he was in love with Helene, the young woman who had nursed him back to health. He gave up the idea of the gold fields, married his nurturing angel of mercy, and settled in the Soda Creek area.

Gertie Dussault was the youngest of ten children, with six brothers and three sisters. One sister married a Curtis of Williams Lake, another married a Lyne at Soda Creek, and the third moved from the Cariboo, marrying and settling in Vancouver.

Gertie, according to old-timers, was a lovely young woman and a talented cook. At sixteen she began working for the Gang Ranch, and when the owners moved, spent a year in Montana with them. Later she worked for the Mickey Martins on the River Ranch in the Chilcotin. Of the latter, she said that she could always tell when Mickey was working up one of his famous thirsts. He paced back and forth for hours in front of the ranch house, leading his horse.

The man that she chose for a husband was not thought to be worthy of her hand. Mike Isnardy remembers that he was an easygoing young cowboy who "was crazy about horses and wasn't around very much." Though horsemanship and

Knife Creek Road at 141 Mile House, eight miles away from where Gertie took a position as housekeeper for Bill Walker.

wanderlust may be attractive qualities in a certain way, they are not high on the list of husbandly virtues. The marriage didn't endure.

Gertie did not have children, and the love that she might have given to her own was transferred to nieces and nephews—particularly the Curtis boys, the Curtis girls Lil, Ollie, and Mabel, as well as Irma and Norma Dussault and the Lynes of Soda Creek.

Gertie became our nearest neighbour when she took over the position of housekeeper for a partially disabled First World War veteran, Bill Walker. He had a small ranch eight miles from 141 Mile House on Knife Creek Road, where he raised a few sheep and cattle. Bill was actually a war hero and fought in the two major battles, Vimy Ridge and Passchendaele in World War I, which defined Canada as a nation.

I remember that my first job was trapping barn rats for Bill. For each tail, I received five cents. My second paying job was picking blueberries. Gertie offered a whole dollar (a fabulous sum in those days) for a ten-pound pail of blueberries. The only drawback to the berry-picking job was that as the blueberries reached the top of the bucket, the level dropped due to dehydration and settled before I could deliver it. I finally presented the bucket of berries, a little short, but Gertie paid me a dollar anyway.

Bill Walker was a laid-back character with a quiet but contrary response to Gertie's antipathy to alcohol. She had seen its devastating effect on her own family. Bill's attitude was much more lenient, and while Gertie lavished brandy on her ailing lambs, Bill was quietly siphoning it and replacing it with tea instead. One day Gertie noted a contaminant in the bottle. There was no doubt that it was a tea leaf, and Bill was harshly reprimanded.

As an ill-conceived joke, someone reported to the police that Gertie was bootlegging homebrew along Knife Creek Road. Three Mounties, their mood influenced by the abominable spring roads, knocked at the door and told Gertie of their suspicions. She was so horrified that she could only silently wave them through the house. The whole event left a lasting scar on the kindly woman, and the culprit escaped unscathed.

Irma and Norma Dussault were nieces who came out to Knife Creek each summer. Gertie nearly lost Norma on one occasion. Norma had been told that if she got lost while riding the range, she should let the horse take the lead and it would bring her home. Sure enough, Norma got lost over by Haley's cabin and true to instruction let the horse have its head. However, the horse was from a different range and Norma was found hours later, many miles from home. So much for horse sense.

Our summer and school holidays were enlivened by hunting and fishing excursions with Gertie's second generation of nephews and nieces. She was a second mother to them and had the magical quality of being able to produce a constant supply of cookies and cakes. That mastery, combined with the freedom of the country, brought this horde to Aunt Gertie's house every school holiday.

When Gertie's mother, Helene Dussault, was over 100 years old, she was brought out to the Knife Creek Ranch where Gertie nursed her to her end two years later. Helene had witnessed both a pre-gold-rush Cariboo and the modern era.

Through the years, the Hills and Paul Ranch and Gertie's Knife Creek Ranch got along well with only a few minor differences. One argument arose over her little black bull, acquired on a three-way trade between the Mayfields of 141 Mile House and ourselves. Hills and Paul Ranch got a good Hereford bull in exchange for a sausage-factory candidate. Gertie, a bit unjustly, got a little black pest who was fiendishly amorous and aggressive. A bit miffed, she let her bull run loose on the range, and the next spring, to our dismay, scrubby black calves arrived in great numbers. This was the complete antithesis to George Mayfield's plan to improve the breeding stock on the range. One of the cowboys from the 141 Mile House came upon the bull on the open range, pulled out his rifle, and shot the bull right there.

In Gertie's later life she moved to Vancouver. Arthritis and other health problems hastened her death in 1963. Ray Curtis, a nephew, observed on her death, "With Auntie gone, who is going to pray for us now?"

CHAPTER 10

LAND OF OPPORTUNITY

Big Claus Mikkelsen of McIntosh Lake

Another pioneer of the Cariboo was Big Claus Mikkelsen. He was a solid Dane, 5' 8" tall, twelve stone, and sturdily built. His pale blue eyes watered, and small veins collected on his ruddy cheeks in response to years of exposure to weather– the bitter cold in winter and the heat of the short summers.

He was born in a small Danish town near Copenhagen and at age sixteen was sent to reside with relatives in the Beavers Valley area of British Columbia. After three weeks of stormy

The Cariboo is full of beaver, and Big Claus took an opportunity that led him into a lot of adventures.

Atlantic weather, the subdued Dane was duly deposited in Montreal and began the Canadian Pacific train journey to the Cariboo. This proved to be a mind-boggling experience, accustomed as he was to pygmy-sized European countries. The two days to cross northern Ontario astounded him, and he thought the Prairies would never end. The Rocky Mountains gave him a crick in the neck, and the bouncing 200-mile coach trip to Beavers Valley from Ashcroft didn't help. When he finally arrived at Beavers Valley, where Little Claus Mikkelsen farmed, he was taken to sturdy Danish bosoms and taught the rudiments of Cariboo ranching.

Here was a land of opportunity, and with few savings, Big Claus homesteaded 160 acres near McIntosh Lake. He acquired a trapline and became a beaver trapper, purchased further meadowland, and gradually added equipment and cattle.

It was at about this time that we became acquainted with Big Claus. His cattle, which should have ranged around McIntosh Lake, sensibly drifted west to escape a steady diet of pea vine and pine grass. That put his multicoloured flock into our herd, and Claus usually spent two or three days on our ranch once or twice a year.

On one occasion while separating his cattle, a two-year-old heifer caught Claus' woollen coat on untrimmed horns, and in her haste pushed him through the open corral gate into the adjacent manure pile. There she proceeded to spread fertilizer through Danish territory. Claus was aggrieved but philosophical. He was inured to cow manure.

Somewhere along the line, the bachelor life lost its allure for Big Claus. Perhaps it was the thought of some little mermaid in Copenhagen harbour, or the Indian lasses that accompanied parents on trapping expeditions, or perhaps Danes don't think of romance until they're 40. But Claus was pining for the soothing voice and soft touch of a woman in his rough-hewn log cabin, sans water, sans electricity, and sans central heat. His thoughts strayed increasingly towards a mate who would make this into a paradise for two.

He did the sensible thing and placed an ad in the paper. In due time a 30-year-old woman with her 9-year-old son arrived from Hatzic in the Lower Mainland. Claus entered wedded life. For the next few years we saw less of Claus but heard indirectly that things were less than idyllic near McIntosh Lake. A visiting cousin was lost in a tragic shooting accident. The stepson, Clayton, had a hard life with lots of work and little schooling. A wire ran from the Mikkelsen bed across the open space to a second cabin. At six each morning Claus seized the wire and gave it a strong pull, ringing the cowbell over his stepson's bed as a signal for him to rise, build a stove fire, tend the stock, and milk the cows.

One day a forlorn twelve-year-old arrived at our porch doorstep at 6 a.m. after an argument at Mikkelsen's home the previous evening. He had walked all night over the forested trails and wagon roads to escape. We fed and cared for the little mite, and he told us he was headed for relatives in the Lower Mainland. When he went on, we notified the police that he was safe. He was retrieved by social workers and sent back to the isolated ranch where the hardships of his life continued. The next time he escaped, a more careful questioning by authorities resulted in separation from his mother and stepfather.

Claus' marriage did not thrive. The few times we saw the couple together, both were tight-lipped and strained. One day two men on horseback came through our ranch and asked for directions to the Mikkelsens. One was Mrs. Mikkelsen's father and the other was her brother. The next day they rode by again with Mrs. Mikkelsen, looking grim and withdrawn. There was no Claus Mikkelsen with them.

What had happened has happened many times. The isolation, the harshness of ranch life, paucity of comforts, and separation from civilization wears. Cabin fever takes over. When the anxiety reaches a crescendo, one has to flee. However, Mrs. Mikkelsen did eventually return, and four children were born to the couple.

I always felt that Claus was not a harsh man. He had few cultural and social skills but was basically decent. Life was hard for him. He was a superb beaver trapper, and the fur trade was still a major industry in B.C. during his lifetime. His catch numbered 100 pelts each spring. Three different trap

Beaver hides stretched and drying.

settings were made, the first by placing two poplar poles together under the ice close to a beaver's house. The beaver, seeing fresh food, was attracted and caught in the trap set on the poles. Death was quick and painless. A second setting was made in the underwater entrance to the houses. The ring on the trap was placed on a pole planted in the bottom of the lake. When the beaver dove into the water, the ring slid down, capturing the beaver and drowning it. The third method was to place a trap on one of the beaver's feeding shelves.

On one occasion Big Claus and his brother shipped a well-finished lot of beaver skins to a competition and won a top prize. On another occasion, while checking his traps five miles away from home in bitterly cold weather, Claus fell through the ice and got soaked in water to his neck. He knew he could not start a fire and would freeze to death if he did not reach his cabin. He set off at a trot and covered the whole five miles. On reaching his cabin he was covered with ice.

Claus taught me how to shoot grouse perched in a tree by taking the lowest one first so that the others wouldn't spook. He showed my brother and me how to set beaver traps under the ice and how to locate keekwillie depressions at McIntosh Lake. He even helped us excavate the rocky ground to find artefacts.

He was talented in the kitchen, although his recipe for cooking beaver tail can't be found in a modern cookbook. The old-timers regarded beaver tail as a delicacy, but now beavers eat the bitter inner layer of deciduous trees, and barbecued beaver tail is absolutely terrible.

Big Claus helped my brother and me with our own culinary difficulties. Our sourdough bread, pancakes, and biscuits would always come out flat and bitter. Again and again we followed Claus' suggestions, without improvement. Finally he hit on the solution: keep the potato water, flour, and yeast mixture warmer. Sure enough, we wrapped the makings in wax paper, put them in bed between our dog and us at night, and the result was perfect sourdough bread, biscuits, and pancakes.

In his later years Claus dabbled in mining and stock ventures, and like many, got into financial difficulties. The bank, which had loaned a considerable amount of money on Claus' estimation of his number of cattle, became suspicious and called Bill Twan to make an independent survey. There was a significant shortfall in the actual number of cattle, and this was a serious matter in the Cariboo. Bankers relied on the word of ranchers, and integrity was vital for the economic welfare of the cattle ranchers. Claus was put in jail and his ranch was repossessed. He died in 1963.

The code of ethics in the Cariboo could be merciless. Mistakes often meant death, and the mistake of being human cost Big Claus his ranch and his freedom. Somewhere inside him was still the overwhelmed sixteen-year-old who had come to the Cariboo so long ago. They say that the meek shall inherit the earth, and perhaps that boy regained his land in a different world. One might even hope that a little Danish mermaid in Copenhagen harbour was there to shed a tear and welcome him to a land of sunshine, fragrant flowers, and perpetual leisure and pleasures.

CHAPTER 11

THE CARIBOO INVENTOR

Orville Fletcher and His Beaver Farm

A s far as I was concerned, Orville Fletcher was the most entrepreneurial and innovative rancher who ever walked the banks of Knife Creek. No one had ever thought to raise beavers on a farm. Orville tried, but with little success.

If anyone was prepared for this wild venture, it was Orville. Of average height and medium build, with straight, fine, light-brown hair and a ruddy complexion, he had been tempered in the school of hard knocks, a foster child placed in a strict old-fashioned German home where the work ethic had long ago won out over such diversions as education, recreation, exhibition of affection, and meaningful discourse. An upbringing

Beaver dam at Squawks Lake, which provided irrigation for thousands of acres of hay land.

of this sort might, in the minds of today's social workers, assure him a place among the have-nots, the socially deprived, or the ne'er-do-wells. On the contrary, he was energetic, innovative, and hardworking, with a great fondness for practical jokes and a contagious, exuberant laugh. As a businessman, he drove a hard bargain but was always honest. Orville had a simple philosophy of "Do for yourself what others would like to do for themselves." After leaving his foster home on the Litzenberg Meadows, nine miles east of 150 Mile House, at age sixteen, he worked at neighbouring ranches. In the back of his mind he was always hoping for a sudden rush of gold so that he could ask his sweetheart, Marie Case, who lived in New York City, to marry him, and he always saved his money just in case the chance for real success came along.

That opportunity came with acquisition of a trapline extending from the San Jose River to the Halfway House on upper Knife Creek, twenty miles east. Four miles from the 141 Mile Ranch, Knife Creek deepened and turned sharply eastward, and sure enough, a family of beavers moved in and built a large dam. The beavers would have enough food supply for years, as the forested land sloped down to the banks of Knife Creek, and aspen and willow trees grew in profusion on either side. As far as Orville was concerned, the possibilities were endless and the time was just right. I am certain that Orville anticipated a bumper crop of beaver skins and fur buyers beating on his door.

Since beavers are wily little rodents and inclined to roam, an enclosing fence was necessary. Orville placed pine logs on top of one another to a height of five feet, securing the end of each panel between two posts. At the critical creek crossings, he used a wire mesh to fill the space between the lower rail of the fence and the bottom of Knife Creek. This was reinforced at the bottom with a steel blade from a road grader. He built a containing fence, encouraged his beavers, and in good humour proceeded with the farm's development. Only one thing stood in the way of his sure-fire success.

The beavers hadn't the slightest intention of being farmed. They squeezed underneath the wire creek barriers, they dug escape holes, and they felled trees onto the fence and disappeared down the creek. The ones that remained on the farm reacted to overcrowding and fought, biting holes in each other's valuable hides. They came down with uncommon diseases such as tularaemia, an infection rarely found in natural surroundings.

The beavers were also victims of enterprising poachers. Since Orville was holding down a full-time job at 150 Mile Ranch, he was not always around to watch his beavers, and poachers reaped a steady toll. Orville had had enough, and he hired his neighbour, Bill Walker, to occupy the small cabin on the bank overlooking the beavers' dam. His job was to act as a protector of the little rodents and to ward off poachers. However, because Bill was a hospitable man and a bit lonely, the poachers paired up and devised a simple strategy where one would visit and drink coffee with Bill while the other slipped off and trapped the beavers. Needless to say, the bodyguard idea was a failure and the beaver farm was abandoned two years later. Orville, realizing his original idea for success did not carry the potential for riches, bought an inexpensive cattle ranch with wild hay meadows sufficient for 300 head of cattle.

Orville may have fit the image of a country bumpkin with a merry laugh and exuberant humour, but women are not always enthralled with tall, dark, and silent men. Ann Miller was such a woman and she was madly in love with Orville, who she referred to as "my little teddy bear." This was perhaps inspired by Orville's thick mat of curly hair on his chest.

Ann had a good job as a schoolteacher and was a stylish young woman. Orville, though flattered by her attention, had lost his heart to Marie years earlier in New York City. Leaving a disappointed Ann (who later rose to a top position in B.C.'s educational system), Orville set out for New York in his 1930 Chevrolet coupe. On arrival he promptly became lost and stopped to ask directions from a policeman. Seeing the B.C. licence plates and eyeing the flustered youth with the ancient Chevrolet, the policeman led him to Marie's door, which was only a block away. The Chevrolet coupe was taken to a nearby garage, where the mechanic suggested that it be taken to the junkyard. Orville tinkered with it instead, and with Marie and her mother and all their luggage, made the return trip of 3000 miles with only one flat tire.

Together at last: Orville and Marie Fletcher of 144 Mile Ranch.

Orville married Marie and they provided a lifelong home for her mother, Mrs. Case. Perhaps she was the mother Orville never knew. He always treated her with affection and respect, and she was an essential part of the family, participating in fun activities, in household duties, and in the care and nurturing of her five grandchildren. In 1949 Orville and Marie took an enormous gamble and bought the 144 Mile Ranch. They dealt in sheep for just long enough to pay off their loan and then switched to cattle. Orville and Marie developed the 144 Ranch to its full capacity, brought in irrigated fields of upland hay, improved their herd by introducing first-class bulls, and used machinery to increase the efficiency of ranch operation.

Orville once found himself in a bidding competition with a wealthy rancher named Riedemann. Orville dearly wanted a prize bull, but the price went beyond his limit. Perspiring profusely and with his last-cent bid, Fletcher looked over at Riedemann and shouted, "Hey, can't you big ranchers give a little guy a break?" Riedemann, slightly embarrassed, brought down his hand and the 144 Mile Ranch had itself a fine bull.

The couple, with the co-operation of Don Gray, built a water-storage dam at Squawks Lake that provided irrigation for thousands of acres of hay land for the 144 and 141 Mile Ranches downstream. Later, Orville invented a device to increase the gripping power of tractor wheels, which was particularly useful on muddy spring roads and wet meadows in haying season. It seemed that in a blink of an eye, Orville had gone from beaver farmer to inventor, but with a lot more success.

Age came, and with it, its infirmities. At 80 years old, the man who had started out as an orphan, abandoned to others' care with little opportunity for education, no capital or family support, and who despite it all had accomplished so much, found it difficult to accept that he could not take his farm with him to the grave. This seems to be the final justice in life. The rich man and the pauper go back to square one with equal fortune.

Near the end, the family, a little uneasy as to Orville's spiritual state, asked their minister to evaluate his chances. The minister spent some time with him and finally came back to the family with these few words: "Leave Orville alone. He's all right."

CHAPTER 12

LOST IN THE NIGHT

Lillian, the Night Walker

Lillian is gone, but then hardly anyone knew she was there. She was always on the other side of an immense wall that cut her off from others, shut her away from the miracle of the sounds of nature and from the voices of people around her. Finally it seemed that she turned towards an inner bubbling of sound that ultimately drove her mad.

Deafness had struck her at ten years old. The cause, I believe, was a viral infection, possibly measles, as everyone else in the family had normal hearing. She was sent away to the Jericho School for the Deaf, where she gained some skill at lip-reading. However, for the most part a great wall of silence separated her from everyone and everything. She never married and had no children. She lived with her mother at Spuzzum, a small settlement on the Fraser River near Yale, B.C. With a small disability pension, she was able to rent an apartment in Vancouver for limited periods of time, and this gave her a break from rural isolation. Even so, her disability and isolated living conditions finally resulted in her becoming withdrawn and depressed. She heard inner voices directing her to do inappropriate things. This behaviour became so increasingly bizarre that she was committed to the mental institution of Essondale. Lillian was what is known as "fay" or "quare" and was similar to the millions of people in the world who don't quite fit in. I always thought that had she been rich, she would have simply been seen as eccentric. People who were penniless as she was, however, have never been allowed much tolerance.

After a time she was discharged from Essondale and came to the Knife Creek Ranch where her brothers, John and Bert Dodd, lived. Her mother Marion was close by, and Lillian was to reside in this Cariboo haven for the next 22 years. John and Bert built a small clapboard cabin for her at the lower end of the pastureland of their ranch, close to Knife Creek and separated from the Disputed Meadow by a Russell fence. She obtained water from Knife Creek, and her heating and cooking facilities were a single wood-burning stove.

The Felker Trail, where most travellers would get lost in the dark. Lillian walked it fearlessly.

And then she started walking—as no one along Knife Creek Road had ever walked before. She walked on the road to the 150 Mile store seventeen miles away, returning with the few groceries she required. She walked the trails that led for miles through the woods, never hearing the sounds of birds or the noises made by wild animals. She was oblivious to the howls of a nearby wolf, the snorting and rattling horns of a bull moose, or the grunts and woofs of a foraging bear.

Then she began to venture out at night. A late-returning range rider coming along a darkened trail would see a dim figure ahead. His horse, picking up the scent of an unfamiliar person, would raise its head, directing its ears towards the new sound as it shied across the trail. Horse and rider would edge warily around the strange apparition, unaware of her condition. Indeed, Lillian could not hear a rider's greeting nor could she lip-read in the darkness. Any cowboy who did touch her soon learned that she fought like a wildcat. There was nothing to do but pass silently as Lillian the night walker continued on her way down the darkened trail.

Only once did her walking get Lillian into trouble. She had followed the road from her house past the Hills and Paul Ranch, then along a trail through the upper pasture. There she found a logging route that wandered through the woods to the Felker Trail, where many secondary paths took off in varying directions.

After a couple of days her absence was noticed, and searchers scattered out to look for her. No one knew which way she had gone, and because she could not hear, the difficulties were staggering. Nine days passed without any sign of her. As hope was fading, Lillian suddenly walked out of the woods at the 150 Mile House, hungry and tired but otherwise well.

She walked less after that. Although we were never sure about what had happened to her, it was as if her spirit had left her. Her night walking was curtailed to short journeys on nearby roads.

In 1975 I saw her for the last time. Lillian was standing outside her cabin door, holding a rifle. She was dressed in worn tennis shoes with no stockings and in a print dress that buttoned down the front with half the buttons undone. She seemed very grim and completely involved in the problem of her runaway dog, which she had resolved to shoot if she could find him.

We took alarm and attempted to console her.

"Not us, ma'am. Believe us, if it was us we wouldn't run off like that dog. We would stick around for sure." We were so taken aback by her anger that we forgot she couldn't hear us and probably could not make out our dismal attempts at calming her down. All the time we were edging away as surreptitiously as possible.

It came as a surprise when after her death a diary was found in her dilapidated cottage. In the diary Lillian had recorded the most perceptive observations of others, beautiful and sensitive thoughts about the world, and her deepest aspirations for her life and future. May all her wishes come true. Blessed are the poor in spirit for theirs is the kingdom, and blessed are the meek for they shall inherit the earth.

CHAPTER 13

THE ICE SPIRIT

Old Herber's Moment of Truth

*N*ot many people wrestle the Ice Spirit. Most people just sit around a warm fire and keep lamps bright to scare the spirit away, but old Herber was hiyu skookum (very great) and not afraid of anything. He stood up to the ice demon, wolf demon, and cold demon and stared them down. He called them by name and spit in their eyes.

It was in the year 1935 that the cold had the country surrounding Knife Creek in its grasp, squeezing and squeezing. That January, every day was -40, the air had little ice bits floating along, the creeks froze to the bottom, and water rose over the ice pans and froze again. At night the dark aspen trees exploded with ear-splitting cracks.

Old Annie would have called it *hiyu solleks*, a very tough time for wildlife. The moose stood humped over, their noses iced, the ends of their guard hairs frosted, trying to eat enough frozen willow twigs to keep a 1000-pound body warm. The little chickadees fluffed up and crowded close to the trunks of pine trees, and the coyotes curled up in the grass underneath the trees, out of the snow, with their noses covered by their tails, dreaming again of their last meal.

Old Herber had had enough, and he shook his fist, saying, "Damn you, cold. I'm not taking this any longer. I'm not going to sit around this stove one more day. I'm free and I'll go where I want when I want. No cold is going to hold me like a prisoner!"

And he meant it. He put on his fleece-lined underwear, his heavy woollen shirt, two pairs of woollen pants, a woollen sweater, and his sheepskin coat. Then he put two pairs of woollen socks on his feet and stepped into his felt boots. Lastly he donned his cap with flaps coming down over his ears and wound a long scarf closely around his neck.

It was two o'clock in the afternoon and the temperature was -48. He chose his saddle horse—not the big gelding, but a little mare called Nancy. She was brown with a white blaze on her forehead. Nancy was fat and had always been fat, and she was usually lazy, but tough. The little mare didn't like the idea of leaving her warm barn and protested against Herber's crazy idea. But he was determined not to let the cold beat him. He put a big sheepskin blanket under the saddle and mounted. The two set off under a pale cold sun towards the mail depot at Enterprise, twelve miles away.

The snow crunched under the mare's hooves as she trotted, her muzzle iced, and her ears and mane frosted. Snow froze to her fetlocks, but still she kept going, braving the elements along with her master. Herber was warmed by her body heat coming through the saddle, but he could feel his face burning and then grow numb and he knew that his skin was freezing.

Three miles on the way, Herber and Nancy stopped off at the Murphy Meadow where Bert Roberts lived in the Old Powers' cabin and fed cattle. He figured that old Herber was *hiyu pelton* (crazy), but brought him in for hot tea and gave Nancy some grain before sending them on their way.

An hour later they arrived at 141 Mile House, which Angus McLauchlin owned at that time. Being a Scot, he knew about the Ice Spirit and he knew that a man's honour was important. He warmed Herber and sent him on down the Old Wagon Road to Enterprise station, the mail drop-off point.

By then it was dark, and Nancy crunched the snow as she skirted the spot on 140 Mile Hill where Clegg was murdered. They trudged on by the 137 Mile, then another half mile to Enterprise railway station, where they picked up two sacks of mail. These letters, magazines, and newspapers meant more than anything to isolated ranch families that were all but cut off from the outside world. Herber tied the sacks firmly behind the saddle. He turned Nancy around, and when they were twelve miles from home, the Ice Spirit tried his hardest to undo Herber's resolution. He seized the two lone figures and squeezed them until they could feel their breath constricting, feel death closing about them in that final sleepiness.

Old Herber knew that this was the greatest test, the moment of truth. He did the only thing he could think of and opened his mouth wide and sang. He sang the songs his mother had taught him, the old Irish ballads, the gospel hymns, even Western songs like "Home on the Range" and "Red River Valley." Nancy heard the songs and somehow knew that they would make it. She made her little feet move more quickly, and they finally reached the warmth of the 141 Mile House. The McLauchlins were worried. They could see that horse and man had been tested almost to the limit. They implored

Old Herber after wrestling with a killer wolf (left). His faithful horse Nancy is below.

old Herber to stay over, but he sensed final victory and turned towards the night for the last eight miles.

At 1 a.m. they reached Murphy's Meadow, where Bert Roberts had waited anxiously in his cabin for them to pass by. After a few minutes Herber continued onward, arriving home at 2 a.m. The temperature was -68.

The fire in the great stove roared, letters and newspapers were read, and Nancy returned thankfully to her warm stall in the barn for fresh hay and grain. The next morning the mercury was frozen in its column at −70 degrees. But the Ice Spirit had been wrestled to the ground and beaten. He slunk away, and a warm Chinook wind soon melted the snow and ice. Old Herber had beat that spirit fair and square.

CHAPTER 14

THE MAN WHO TALKED TO HORSES

Charles Isnardy

In isolated settings, a special relationship develops between human and animal. In some cases these relationships begin to take on almost-human characteristics. Most people would say that no one can speak to horses, but I was a witness to Charlie's gift, and furthermore, to the fact that the horses talked to him.

It all started when his father, Amedee Isnardy (Amedee, translated from Basque, means one who loves God), left the Pyrenees region of France in 1854. With two brothers he boarded a ship bound for Mexico. It's likely that fourteen-year-old Amedee thought Mexico was a country much like his native Pyrenees, with a similar language. When he was disabused of this notion, he left Mexico for California, pursuing gold, and ended up in the southern Cariboo. He

Charles Isnardy
c. 1906.

*Amedee Isnardy's home, after a
saloon was added in the early 1900s.*

stopped for a time at Lillooet, where he met a Salish princess,
Julliene Wilamatkwa, who took the eye, heart, and name of
the migrant herder with foreign ways and atrocious speech.
The two settled in Chimney Creek, twenty miles west of 141
Mile House. They had eight children.

The fourth child was Charlie, born in 1872, and his
beginning days were spent in silence. There was no one for
Charlie to talk to because his father spoke Basque and only
broken English, his mother spoke Salish, and Joseph, Frances,
and Awtencia spoke whatever seemed to fit.

So Charlie spoke to the horses, Bruno and Jorge, in the
evenings. Their whickering sometimes seemed to say "Hello
Charlie," and at this, the solemn brown-eyed boy climbed up
on the manger and sat on the railing between the stalls. After
placing their evening meal in the manger, Charlie would pat
each horse on its soft nose as they bowed their heads to take a
mouthful of hay. And so Charlie, through the years, learned to
talk to the horses and the horses talked to Charlie.

Charlie grew into a barrel-chested, swarthy young man
who showed both Mediterranean and Native ancestry. A
drooping handlebar moustache set off his twinkling brown eyes.
He was powerfully built and had the rolling gait of one used to
the saddle. He had a soft voice and teased the teenaged ranch
boys about girls on neighbouring ranches. With ladies he was
courtly and attentive, and generally made agreeable company.

However, Charlie never married. He spent his time telling adventure stories with the utmost solemnity. He told of experiences in South Africa during its war with Britain, daring hunting events with grizzly bears, and near escapes in bronco riding exhibitions.

He told of a time when a *cheechaco* (newcomer) in a local bar accosted him. The loudmouthed inebriate challenged everyone within hearing distance.

"I can lick anyone in this bar."

Then "I can lick anyone in this town." No one responded. "I can lick anyone in this province."

Charlie walked up and gave him one blow that supposedly flattened him.

"I guess you took in a little too much territory that time," he reportedly said mildly.

Most of Charlie's stories were complete fabrications. He invariably turned out to be a minor hero, but they harmed no one. There may have been a lifted eyebrow or a wink in response, but in general his accounts were accepted with good humour.

It was Charlie's habit of talking with the horses that attracted most of the attention. He would say to his favourite horse, "Babe, you are a splendid animal, a fine riding horse. You are in fact the best horse in this whole durn country." And Babe whickered in pleasure and gave Charlie a great slobbery kiss that left one or the other of his magnificent handlebar moustaches wet and drooping. He also had kind words for his two pack horses, Jose and Villa, each of whom carried 200 pounds of grain on the 40-mile return trip from Chimney Creek.

All the horses talked with Charlie, particularly Babe, a notoriously good judge of men. As far as anyone could tell, she thought Charlie belonged on a throne somewhere, with a halo above his head.

Charlie called the Isnardy Ranch on Chimney Creek home, although he worked around the Springhouse area. After his father's death in 1908, he inherited land but relinquished it to a brother. Later he bought land far up Knife Creek Road on the 108 Mile Road, two miles past the fingerboard directional

Charlie and his horse Villa, who seemed to agree with Babe that Charlie was an angel with horses.

sign on the road to Murphy Lake. It wasn't much of a ranch, only 160 acres, a quarter of which was swamp meadow. But Charlie built a one-room log cabin and, nearby, a flat-roofed barn. The horse barn, twenty square feet, had flattened logs for flooring and poles overhead for a roof. Swamp hay laid over those poles provided a water barrier against summer rain and winter snow.

The cabin itself was not palatial. It had a sod roof, a rough board floor, a bed set along the back wall, a stove in the front corner, and a washstand under the front window. There were no amenities like water or indoor plumbing. Rather, there was a shallow well at the edge of the meadow, and a small shanty at the back of the cabin sufficed for a washroom. The cabin floor was littered with the detritus of ranch life: bits of harness, a saddle in the process of repair, horseshoes, cans of nails, tools, grain sacks, saddles, medicines for his horses, and tin boxes containing various useful items. There seemed to be established trails across the floor, from door to bed, bed to stove, and stove to washstand. Large nails driven into logs by the door served as coat hangers.

Charlie wasn't concerned with the comforts of living. It was the simple range cayuse of the Cariboo that he loved. He would pet them, talk to them, and fuss over them. At timely intervals he trimmed their hooves, combed and thinned their tails, and in summer rubbed lard into raw areas left by swarms of black flies, no-see-ums, and mosquitoes. He also built smudge fires to ward off insect pests so that his horses could rest and gain relief from their tormentors. Charlie had another treat in store for his horses—he fed them grain. This was in a country where most cayuses never saw a kernel of grain in their lifetime. In winter, most pawed through the snow for frozen swamp grass, and in summer they grazed on upland grasses, but Charlie's horses feasted on real grain.

People love horses, but most horses don't love people. One day Charlie was training a new and skittish pony to the halter. Later, friends searching for him found him lying in the middle of the corral with the horse trotting round and round, halter rope dragging behind. In the centre of the corral lay Charlie, dead, his chest crushed by thundering hooves, his hand holding an overturned pail containing a horse's ration of grain.

In the end I'm sure I heard Babe say it best. "There will never be another man as good as Charlie."

Will Charlie's legend carry on? I think so. A grandniece, years later, said to me, "Uncle Charlie, he was such a nice man. And did you know he talked with his horses?"

The deserted cabin at
Charles Isnardy's place.

CHAPTER 15

UNLINED POCKETS, SHALLOW GRAVES

An Unmarked Grave at Nelly's Lake

This is a sad story, a reflection on a horrifying time in Canadian history that is all but forgotten in the present comparatively affluent way of life. The Great Depression of the "Dirty Thirties" from 1930 to 1938 was a desperate time when the spirit of the land was almost sapped away. Economic disaster lay all about, and with it came a national depression of spirit. There were no worthwhile jobs, practically no money, and families were fractured. Without a way of supporting themselves, people resorted to desperate measures. Men and women sold their labours for any return that provided bare survival. Twenty-five cents a day plus food and a miserable straw mattress in a shack was a standard wage. Many thought themselves lucky to have even this.

Reverend Stanley Herber, one of the argonauts, now aged 81 years, lives in an idyllic setting amidst orange, grapefruit, and avocado trees in San Diego, California. But in the Cariboo in 1936 he endured, as did most small-time ranchers, the most straitened of circumstances. He remembers that there was no money, that five dollars was a small fortune. A salary of 100 dollars per month was a princely wage. He reminds me that civil servants who received a steady income of 80 dollars a month were the most fortunate individuals in the area and could afford a new car every year or two.

The final resting place of an unknown man.

In June of 1936, he was range riding with Harry Barnard ("Barney") for wild horses across the railway near Nelly's Lake. (This small lake lies four miles west from 130 Mile House on Highway 97.) Tired and thirsty, they arrived at a small log cabin surrounded by scrub poplar and scattered pine trees. There was not even an outhouse. A strange and ominous silence lay about the dwelling. No livestock was visible, and the door of the cabin, made up of barley sacks, hung limply. A lone window was covered with a dirty white flour sack. No smoke came out through the top of a rusty stovepipe.

The riders dismounted from their horses and shouted, seeing if someone was around. There was no response. Barney pushed aside the sacking and cautiously made his way into a barely furnished single room. In one corner was a crude bed constructed of poles and covered with a blanket. Underneath the blanket lay the emaciated body of a man in the advanced stages of decomposition. There was no food or water to be found.

The riders dug a shallow grave behind the cabin, folded the blanket over the man's remains, carried him outside, and buried him in a lonely grave without even a wooden cross.

This done, they mounted their horses, continuing their hunt for the wild horses of Nelly's Lake.

There was no means of identifying the man, no letters from a wife, no pictures of loved ones. Somewhere in Canada or the United States, a family or perhaps a spouse may have wondered where a lost one had ended his days.

In the Great Depression, life was cheap and death was sometimes the only means of escape. Most of us who heard about the wretch in the cabin knew that this had been the way for him. No old-timer of the Cariboo has been able to shed much light on this unfortunate man. Somehow I draw comfort from the poet William Cullen Bryant in these lines from *To A Waterfowl*:

> He who from zone to zone
> Guides through the boundless sky
> Thy certain flight
> In the long way that I
> must tread alone
> Will lead my steps aright.

CHAPTER 16

DEATH WAS THE MORNING HUNTSMAN

An Accidental Death Near Spout Lake

Since Creation, man has gone forth in the morning to hunt and to till the soil, and at the end of the day some don't come home. Thus it was that on a sunny October morning, four hunters came through the Hills and Paul Ranch, and only three came back. The oldest, Johnson, was seated on the supply wagon. Three others rode beside him, leading pack horses. We watched them at the gates, how they were all filled with the joy of the hunt and each burned with the vibrant energy of youth. Animated talk and laughter flowed back and forth, and their horses, too, stood straight and proud. From time to time they thrust their heads forward, tightening their reins and clattering their bridle bits, impatient to be on the way. After a few words of greeting, the hunting party was gone. The open barnyard gates closed behind them and dust rose lightly from the hooves of the horses and the turning wheels of the wagon as they made their way up the narrow road.

That night they made camp by Spout Lake near the McIntosh Mountains. Supper was prepared over a campfire, and pine boughs laid as cushion beds. Nearby the tethered horses cropped grasses while the moon, rising above Boss and Timothy Mountains, made its way across the sky. In the distance a lone wolf cried, and on a nearby spruce tree an owl sounded a message of impending tragedy.

The hunt began in the dim light of early morning, even before a thought was given to food or drink. With guns at the ready, the silent hunters walked stiffly in single file through the grass and low kinnikinik plants, leaving a trail in the morning dew. They reached their destination, a half-mile distance from the overnight camp. A swampy meadow dotted with clumps of buckbrush lay under a low, drifting morning mist, which obscured the far margin of willows.

One by one the hunters dropped to their knees behind clumps of branches to await the coming of a moose. When the dawn drove away the mist, and the light of the sun below the horizon chased the darkness, an explosive grunting and a clatter of horns against willow shards sounded from the far side of the meadow. Suddenly a bull moose burst onto the marsh. He stood by the willow margin, head high, horns set

The owl, thought to warn of tragedy, sounded its call the night before the hunt.

back, challenging all. The hunters could do nothing except gaze, and one by one they slipped the safety catches on their rifles, each taking steady aim. The gunsights lined up on the point behind the angle of the beast's shoulder. One finger tightened on a rifle's trigger, then squeezed.

At that moment, a crouching Johnson, positioned slightly forward of the rest, raised his head—to get a better look or to gaze longer at the magnificent moose, no one is sure. But a shot burst across the morning stillness, echoing and re-echoing from tree to hill and mountain and back again. Johnson pitched forward, dead, propelled by the impact of the bullet striking the back of his head.

The first news of the tragedy came with the arrival of a single hunter at the outer gate of our ranch. The haggard rider dismounted and led his spent and heaving horse through the gate. "Johnson's dead, killed this morning. Got to get to town to tell someone," the rider said, his voice hoarse and breaking. "The rest of the boys will be along with the wagon."

"You aren't going to go any further on that horse," we told him. "Come in and get some breakfast and tell us what happened."

We remembered him as one of the hunters who had passed by so carefree and excited with the chase such a short time before. He now stood exhausted, unshaven, covered with lather from the horse, every action and word telling of his sorrowful burden. The horse as well, straight and tall as he'd left for his journey was now sagging with exhaustion, head drooping, hair matted with lather. We removed the saddle and walked the animal, giving it a small amount of water and food.

We gave the rider breakfast and comforted him as best we could before dispatching him the 28 miles to Williams Lake. At four o'clock the wagon arrived with dust billowing. The horses and men were strained and exhausted. We who had never seen death approached the wagon with dread, even as we greeted the men and waved them to our home. We cared for the horses but could not take our eyes off our first sight of the terrible stillness of death under the canvas sheet on the wagon bed.

Johnson was gone and his proud spirit would never be on the land again. No human wish could restore to life the carefree individual who had so blithely gone forth to the hunt the previous day. The mournful lines from an old Scottish lay that bespoke a similar sadness seemed to fit then as they had so many centuries before:

All saddled and bridled and booted rode he,
To home came his lead horse, but never came he.

CHAPTER 17

REAL HEROES AND COWBOYS

John Dodd, War Hero of Knife Creek Road

Through my years I've been very aware of the oldest emotions of mankind, emotions like vengeance, aggression, and covetousness, which spring straight from the primeval swamp of the human id. This seething cesspool is layered over by a thin veneer of civilization, without which these behavioural instincts would be open and raging. For this reason the Cariboo's own hero in the cauldron of war has a fatal attraction and is of particular interest. He came from Knife Creek Road, with its open spaces, mountains, and lakes, and its tranquil rural life. There should have been little to prepare him for a fierce conflict in Europe, where soldiers were often moulded by age-old traditions of warfare and historical grievances. John Dodd wasn't motivated by these reasons. Rather, he was driven by a desire to avenge his father's death in World War I and by a need for adventure.

I first met him in 1936 when he was hired at the 141 Mile Ranch. His widowed mother had raised him in the small Fraser Canyon community of Spuzzum, with his brother Bert and his sister Lillian (see chapter 12). His father had been killed in action in World War I, and John had pledged vengeance ever since. On arrival, however, he seemed far from anyone's ideal of an aspiring war hero. He was shy and inexperienced and seemed set on being a cowboy and learning the cattle ranching trade. Although sturdily built, he had a clear, pink complexion and a tendency to blush and stammer when excited, which belied his physical strength and well-developed, muscular arms and legs. This strength was to serve him in good stead when he later became a champion rodeo rider. In a relatively short time he developed into a first-rate horseman, a skill complemented by a natural instinct for animal husbandry.

There were a number of high-spirited men at the 141 Mile House besides Johnny. There was Roland Mayfield, Marvin Mayfield, Johnny's brother Bert, Louis Bates, Carl Eldie, and Melvin Mayfield. They spent their time riding for cattle on the range that lay east of the Cariboo Highway, putting up hay during the summer, repairing fences during the spring and fall, and feeding the cattle during the six months of winter.

There was a light-hearted deviltry that went on between them. One would ride up alongside another's placid mount and toss a lariat end to a second boy, who ran the rope under the tail of the mount of the unsuspecting rider. The resulting fishtailing and bucking made for whoops of laughter amongst the others, particularly if the rider was unseated.

On one occasion a bear was chased up a spruce tree in the 141 pasture. Marvin Mayfield bet Johnny five dollars that he couldn't knock it down. Johnny took the bet, climbed up the tree, and grabbed the bear's hind leg. The bear, immensely startled, let out a "woof" and slid to the ground, with the equally startled cowboy landing on top of it. Man and bear scampered in opposite directions, but in that minute we had all glimpsed the sort of bravery that others would recognize in John Dodd years later.

When 1938 came around, the boys of the 141 Mile House were spoiling for a fight. In October of that year, when Hitler gave Czechoslovakia his ultimatum, they packed their horses and went back to Timothy Mountain for grizzly bear hunting. The group had formed a firm resolve to join the army and take Adolf down a peg when they returned.

As it turned out, they shot no grizzly bear, and Hitler was apparently appeased, much to everyone's disgust. There was a general feeling that the British were shirking their responsibilities to fight for what was right and that if this kept up, there wouldn't be an opportunity to take on Hitler after all. Later they were all to get their bellies full of war, and it wasn't going to be the picnic that they had imagined.

Although the war started in 1939, it did not come to the Cariboo until 1940. When it did, five boys from 141 Mile House ranch joined up. John had recently got himself into trouble with a miffed husband, who had found Johnny with his wife on the second floor of a Williams Lake dwelling. Johnny reasoned that if he was going to get shot, it might as well be by the Germans, who were probably the poorer marksmen. This event sparked the heels of the boy towards battle, who knew that he had to avenge his father's death and quell the yearning to be a hero that burned in his veins.

D-Day in 1944 found John and Roland Mayfield in the first wave of the invasion. After four days of confused fighting, John lay along a hedgerow at dawn, tired, homesick, and separated from his outfit. His attention was directed to a cow in a nearby field that was bawling miserably and pleading to be milked. Sensing something familiar at last, he began to crawl out to milk the cow. As he did, he saw a form crawling from the opposite side of the field. Johnny waited, ready to shoot any enemy that crossed his path. Then he heard another familiar sound. It was the voice of his friend Roland, pleading with him not to shoot. Johnny laughed and lowered his gun. "Is that you Rol?" he said. It proved to be a last talk with his friend, who was wounded the next day and evacuated to England

The months and years went by as John continued fighting, making his way through Normandy and Holland. Tony Foster, in his book *The Meeting of Generals*, tells of Corporal Dodd standing behind a bridge pillar, shouting taunts at the Jerrys on the far bank and spraying them with automatic rifle fire between peals of laughter. This was either war frenzy or a man meant for the circumstances of war. Later he was mentioned in dispatches, performing such deeds as charging an enemy machine-gun nest single-handed and killing or capturing the enemy soldiers. For this particular deed he received the Military Medal for Heroism, pinned on his tunic

by no less than General Bernard Montgomery. Promoted to
sergeant, he finished the war leading his platoon from one
firefight to another. He himself received a crease from a
German bullet and carried a white scar along his temple for
the rest of his days, a reminder that a man may be heroic, but
is never invincible.

During John's time in England, a wartime romance had
blossomed with Pat Grainger, an English woman who worked
as a conductor on a double-decker bus in war-blitzed London.
Pat came to the Cariboo as a war bride in 1947, and I remember
driving Johnny and Pat up to their Knife Creek Ranch, now

John Dodd, accepting the M.C.
from General Montgomery.

called the Dodd Place. It was pouring rain, the narrow road was streaming with water, and we became stuck in mud holes on several occasions. I knew that if Pat could accept this, she might last in the often hostile environment of the Cariboo. She did last for ten years but couldn't take it any longer than that. She ended up settling in Vancouver.

The ranch at Knife Creek did not prosper. John sold his cattle and accepted a position as cow boss at the Chilko Ranch, later moving on to the Gang Ranch. Finally, seeking a change, he went as a cow boss to a large Alberta spread.

Six children were left to carry on the line of the Cariboo's wartime hero. Unlike John, they didn't know the desire for vengeance for a killed father. Rather, they basked in the sun of his honour and bravery, although they never knew John as a soldier. They knew him only as a real Cariboo cowboy.

CHAPTER 18

VOWS AND HAY BALES

Racehorse Johnson and Rita Cunningham

R acehorse Johnson was driven, not to drink but to sobriety, by a pretty western lass from 74 Mile House. Born in 1895, Eric Johnson was the second son of a wealthy English Midlands family. Because of the tradition of primogeniture, there was little likelihood of his succession to large estates in England, but he did receive a healthy maintenance allowance. Whether a fondness for Scotch whiskey (he was fond of it) or a too great

Rita knew that marriage was about cooperation in the Cariboo. Would Johnson be able to give up drink?

familiarity with the village lasses (he was fond of them too) was the reason for his immigration to Canada, we are not sure. But in 1926 he came to British Columbia and bought the 141 Mile Ranch from the Enterprise Cattle Company. This was a 2500-acre ranch, a substantial spread. He wanted to raise magnificent racehorses and make his own fortune. Only a few things stood in his way.

He established himself and, knowing little about cattle ranching, did the prudent thing and hired a knowledgeable Scot, Don Laidlaw, to manage the ranch. Like most English country gentry, Johnson had little talent for cooking and with equal prudence engaged a venerable Chinese relic from the gold-rush days named Bing Chow to manage the old Murphy household.

His next task was to construct a three-quarter-mile racetrack in the flat area of his meadow. It was here that his racing string was to be developed. Eric Johnson was not the right size to be a jockey. He was above average height, somewhat fleshy, with a full, red face, almost choleric, with the early breaking of small veins on his face, likely a legacy of his alcohol intake. He had a straight pencil-thin moustache and pale blue watery eyes. Although pleasant, some found him detached, and he favoured the garb of a conservative country gentleman with chequered hat, whipcord riding trousers, three-quarter-length car coat, and tan shirt open at the neck, as though he wanted to separate himself somewhat from what must have seemed the dirty lifestyle of ranching. His feet were elegantly shod with flat-heeled riding boots, which despite much cleaning, often bore evidence of Cariboo mud.

His riding stable needed a good jockey to train and race his horses. Don Laidlaw was diminutive but too old. Chow was obviously not a candidate. There was no local male to fit the bill. It was then that a flash of inspiration came to him. He had seen a girl riding like the wind at the rodeo in Williams Lake— Rita Cunningham, who lived at 74 Mile House.

She was slim and tall with straight, shoulder-length blond hair and had ridden horses since she was a child on the family ranch. Some people disapproved of the fact that she rode astride the saddle rather than in sidesaddle, considered more

Rita Cunningham,
who both made
and broke a man.

appropriate for ladies. Eric didn't care about things like that, however, and he asked her to ride his horses for him. She agreed. By this time, Eric Johnson had acquired Pale Hands, a prized Thoroughbred stallion, as well as five well-bred mares. His horses raced at Williams Lake, Quesnel, and Prince George.

Rita rode well on a Western saddle but could not achieve the classical riding posture of a jockey on a flat saddle, nor did she ride with shortened stirrups, which might have brought her weight up over the horses' withers. Still she was a natural rider, and Johnson's horses had some success.

Johnson never backed away from a race and fulfilled every challenge except once, when he visited his friend "Doc" Gerald Rumsey Baker, also a lover of good horseflesh. Johnson, a Christmas holiday guest at the Bakers' in Quesnel, consumed a good deal of alcohol with his host. They became involved in a lengthy dispute over the relative merits of their respective horses. The only solution was a race. Their horses would run immediately and settle the matter once and for all. The problem was that two feet of snow lay on the ground outside and it was -40. The race could not be run. They decided to get more drunk instead, and Johnson, then in a considerable pique, got into trouble with the law when he was found pounding on the door of the liquor store at 2 a.m., demanding that it open up and serve the needs of honest citizens. Doc Baker pacified the police and smuggled Eric out of town with Alice and Wayne Herber, who happened to be returning to Knife Creek after the Christmas holidays. On the way home, their 1928 Ford sedan stalled near 153 Mile House, and Racehorse Johnson nearly froze to death in the back seat.

There is something about horses, horse lovers, and hay bales that arouses basic instincts between a man and a woman, and thus it came about that the unspoiled maiden of the West and the older and worldly Eric Johnson developed deeper feelings than normally exist between jockey and owner. Johnson coveted this unsophisticated maiden, who was twenty years his junior and happened to be fond of him. He wished her hand in marriage, but she, with an instinctive feminine shrewdness, knew in her heart that while love was sweet, marriage was a serious business and many obstacles lay in their way.

At Johnson's suggestion, Rita wrote a letter to the family back in England, introducing herself. The response from England was decidedly lukewarm and showed little friendliness or enthusiasm. While this was going on, Racehorse Johnson, feeling the strain, went on a tremendous alcoholic binge that lasted a whole week. These developments decided Rita. She turned down Johnson's proposal and broke his heart. He returned to England, a rejected and forlorn man. On sober reflection he recognized his life's shortcomings, particularly the destructive effect of whiskey on his life. He made a vow of sobriety, gave up the bottle, and turned his life around. During World War II he served with distinction and subsequently entered politics in a Manchester riding and was elected to Parliament in 1951, a Conservative sweeping to power in a Labour stronghold. Bob Beauchamp, the proper, reserved notary public in Williams Lake, sent a three-word congratulatory telegram—"Ride 'em cowboy."

Many years later, as an old man, Eric Johnson returned for a last visit to the Cariboo. His horses were long dead, the racetrack returned to meadow, and his young exciting filly, Rita Cunningham, now an older woman and married to someone else. Perhaps what-ifs occurred to him, and perhaps a greater wisdom consoled him: that one should never try to return to past loves and lives.

CHAPTER 19

DEMONS AND CAULDRONS

Roland and Joyce, A Love That Couldn't Be

Although remote, the central Cariboo and Knife Creek area were not immune to the passions and fortunes of the greater world. Love can exist anywhere and for anyone, a fact proven true by this story.

Many years ago there lived a handsome, gentle, seventeen-year-old young man named Roland, and three miles away, at the 144 Mile Ranch, a comely, brown-eyed young woman named Joyce. They fell in love, and it was a love that was tender and deep, but through the clash of family prejudices and the crucible of war, it was to lead to sorrow and disaster. As often happens in such situations, both innocent and erring became victims.

The two lovers met furtively at first. Roland, at the 141 Mile House, would retire early to his room after evening dinner on the pretext of being weary from the day's labour. Once in his room, he would slip out the gable window of the upstairs bedroom, make his way to the barn, find his horse, and ride the three miles to spend time with Joyce. Of course this could not go unnoticed, and it became a matter of active comment among the family and employees of the ranch, particularly when Roland took his sheepskin coat with him to bed.

Roland's parents were not thrilled by this relationship. They liked Joyce, who was pleasant and attractive. That is, they liked her as a friend but did not favour her as a daughter-in-law. Two things were responsible for this feeling. The first was that she was a Roman Catholic and their family was "hard-shell" Baptists. The second was that Joyce's great-grandmother was a native Salish woman, which made Joyce a quarter Indian by descent. In days when race was so important, it was accepted that a drop of Indian blood made an Indian, and Roland's parents simply could not accept an Indian for a daughter. They set out to break up the love affair, which they soon did. Who knows in what underhanded ways this was

Roland and Joyce—would they ever be together?

accomplished, but the wedge that would develop between the two lovers became almost visible.

When Roland went off to war in 1941, he still held in his heart a deep love for Joyce. Joyce grieved, but, determined to get on with her life, married a cattle rancher who remained out of the war as an essential worker. This rancher had adored her for years but was plain and had little education. Joyce tried to be a good wife. She maintained a neat home and bore two children. Still, there was no way she could completely hide her love for Roland, and her husband sensed it. That she loved another man was like a hot iron burning in his very soul. He became short-tempered and jealous. Roland was lucky that he was not around to face this man's rage, as it would have surely killed one of them.

The war ended, and in September 1945, Roland arrived home. He had been wounded in Normandy on his sixth day of battle. On evacuation to England, his life had been saved by penicillin, and he spent months in a British hospital before he was returned to his unit in Holland. In a shipboard interview, a reporter quoted him as saying: "My one wish is to get my feet under the ranch dinner table again." What was not said was written in letters to his parents during his hospital stay in England.

"When I get home I am going to marry Joyce and nothing will stop me. Don't you dare try."

The boys came home to bands and cheers and rejoicing. Those who had lost loved ones grieved, but still rejoiced with others. It was a deliriously happy event. The returning soldiers were conquering heroes and on their return were taken to the hearts of the Canadian people.

Roland went through a series of brief, loveless relationships, including one with his cousin Miles' wife. Then came the cataclysmic event that led to so much tragedy and heartbreak. Joyce packed up, took her children, and joined Roland on his new ranch at the Murphy Meadow. Her husband, George Felker, was heartbroken and Roland's family was upset, but nothing could be done. Perhaps it was accepted that this was fated to be from the time of their teenage love, a love that had been unsuccessfully blocked by circumstances beyond their control.

Life should have evolved in a happy vein for Roland. The war was over, and with a government grant and family help he had acquired a sizeable ranch. Best of all, he was united with Joyce, the love of his life. Several years passed and children arrived. Outwardly he seemed to be the old Roland—gentle, obliging, and cheerful. But the demons of five years of army life, of injury, of combat experiences, of resentment that he had been separated from the woman he loved, gnawed at him inside. Booze and other women got to him. The love that had inspired him through the years dimmed, and he increasingly became surly and argumentative at home. Finally he disappeared, severing all connections with the family and ranch life that had held such promise.

Joyce possessed a truly heroic durability and carried on, raising the children and eventually remarrying. Roland never came back. Years later a son found him, an old ranch worker in Alberta, completely alone. His father told him bluntly, "Son, go home and don't come back. Don't ever try to find me again. I don't exist to you."

The love between a man and a woman is not simple. Add a war, battle wounds, and years of separation and the mix becomes a witch's cauldron. This anonymous poem speaks to it:

> Of all the words of tongue and pen,
> the saddest are "It might have been."
> Sadder still we daily see:
> It is but shouldn't ever be.

CHAPTER 20

CHERRY PIE AND CHILDREN

Hazel's Spring Estrous Cycle

L ove exists in many forms in the central Cariboo. There was the unrequited love of Racehorse Johnson and Rita Cunningham, and the tragic love of Roland and Joyce. There were the marriages that worked and the marriages that didn't.

And then there was Hazel Rowan. For many years she lived on Knife Creek Road, an unusual woman held captive by nature's rhythms, who went into an estrous cycle each spring. The events were so bizarre and scandalous that my mother, 60 years later, still blushes when reminded. In an isolated cabin in the central Cariboo, Hazel, a 30-year-old married woman, went into a mating frenzy each May. For a month she would play the field of local available males before finally pairing off with a single partner. A week was spent in constant association with this male, and after that week he was discarded and ignored.

How did men know that she was in estrous? In the animal kingdom, females emit pheromones that can be detected by males from a great distance, and these pheromones signal that the female is ready to mate. Can behaviour in the human female be equated with that of females in the animal kingdom? Apparently male apes alter behaviour when in proximity to women in the fertile phases of their cycles, and recent studies confirm that women emit powerful pheromones when in estrous. Men certainly knew when Hazel was receptive.

She had four children spaced at exact intervals, and each February saw a further addition, so there was little doubt as to her fertility. Hazel was full-figured, not unattractive, with curly dark hair, sensuous lips, generous breasts, and in spite of her pregnancies, well-proportioned hips and abdomen.

Hazel's husband, Ernest Rowan, was an insignificant sort of a man. An ailing back, the result of being in the service, kept him from any useful employment. The family existed on his war pension. The household dwelt in a four-room log house beside Knife Creek Road, four miles from 141 Mile House. The structure was without any amenities; wood-burning stoves were used for cooking and heating, water was carried in pails from a nearby well, and sanitary facilities existed in an outdoor privy behind the house. The only luxury was a large Chandler Sedan, which sat for years in front of the house and served as a reminder to anyone who saw it of more affluent times.

Hazel's early life may give some clues to her behaviour. She was essentially orphaned at age ten, her mother confined permanently to a mental institution. Her father was out of the picture. She was bounced from one foster home to another, where there was little love and security and there were some allegations of sexual abuse. When she was twelve years old, she ran away from her foster home and obtained work helping in the kitchen of a logging camp. Usually the workers in a logging camp, while gruff in manner and talk, are genuine and would normally rally around a young girl and give her some protection. Hazel was likely precocious and promiscuous by this time and little could be done for her. She was still twelve years old when she became pregnant, and she gave up the baby for adoption when she was thirteen. Later she married the much older and ineffectual Ernest.

The first May it was Eddy, a young bachelor. For a solid week, Hazel and Eddy were constantly together. They could be seen riding stirrup to stirrup, holding hands, and exploring each other. All this was heavy duty for observant teenagers, which would be a suitable description of the two Lee boys at that time. One day while on a riding expedition for cattle, we saw two horses by a stand of trees, leisurely cropping the grass. In the shadows, two saddles lay on the ground supporting two

Knife Creek Road held many secret coves for young lovers.

figures engaged in frenetic activities. Our retreat was made in considerable haste, silently and with tumultuous thoughts. Following this eye-opening event, vivid images fired our imaginations for days.

The next February saw an addition to Hazel's family, and in May the scenario was repeated with Alec, the brother of Eddy. Next there was Bill, and the following year saw David as the chosen mate. Mother was alarmed and gave her boys instructions to stay away from this woman and have nothing to do with her.

Sexual information was delivered to us by observant uncles who explained Hazel's expanding figure. It was the result, they said, of eating dried apples and the water that Alec was giving her to drink. This was the extent of sex education on Knife Creek Road.

One warm June day I rode my horse by the log house that accommodated Hazel's ever-growing family. I could smell fresh cherry pie. Her husband, Ernest, saw me hot and tired and must have known that as a teenager, I would be ravenously hungry. Walking out to the roadside he said, "Hazel would like to invite you in."

Cherry pie sounded really good, but Mother's very specific instructions won the moment. "I'm not getting off this horse," I said.

Ernest looked perplexed. Then, holding up one finger, he retired inside. He returned a moment later with a large piece of the most delicious cherry pie. Without leaving my saddle, I ate every crumb. I thanked Ernest. "Give my thanks to Hazel," I added. "She is very kind and generous." And she was.

I have thought since of the matter. "Was she an adulterous harlot bent on seducing, or was she a just, kind, loving person in spite of much suffering in her life?" In spite of her many hardships she had maintained an inner kindness. That June day it was kindness that prompted her to take notice of a ravenous boy and send him a large piece of her cherry pie. Mother was wrong this once.

CHAPTER 21

THE QUIET PRIEST

Father William J. Murphy of Knife Creek Road

Like Hannah of biblical times, Irish mothers used to dedicate their first male offspring to the church. Thus it was no surprise that the eldest son of Dennis and Ellen Murphy of 141 Mile House on Knife Creek Road went from being William Joseph Murphy, rancher, to Father William Murphy, O.M.I. Surprisingly, at one time in his life he lived for both of his vocations, an unusual event in the annals of the priesthood.

William Murphy was born in April 1865. No doctor was present for his birth, and his mother was attended by a midwife. Ellen Murphy was the product of thousands of years of strong birthing women. She had ample frame and good pelvic width, but at 25 years of age she was a little old for a first baby. It's likely that Old Annie Basil was the midwife for William since she was the midwife for Denis, born three years later. Mary Felker, with some experience in delivering babies, had not yet arrived at 144 Mile House.

William thrived and survived all the hazards of the first years without immunization against diphtheria, whooping cough, tetanus, and polio and likely was not vaccinated against smallpox, although this disease had wiped out Salish villages west of the Fraser. At that time there were no bathtubs or showers available, and a wash in a galvanized tub was given each weekend whether needed or not. It was common practice for mothers to catch rainwater for hair washing.

William took a full share in ranch chores from an early age. The Murphys' chicken run immediately behind the main dwelling held 80 chickens, and in peak laying season each hay nest held six to ten eggs, which meant about six dozen eggs a day.

The future oblate priest took his early schooling at St. Joseph's Mission, six miles away. The Felkers, who were schoolmates, lived two miles from St. Joseph's Mission and were able to go back and forth each day, but the Murphys found it necessary to board at the Mission school. On Friday evening a horse and carriage brought them home to the ranch where they were expected to do their share of the chores.

During the summer vacation, each boy helped in the milking of eight to ten cows. They would start milking at seven in the morning and again at seven in the evening. The milk cows were herded into the barn, their necks secured between two vertical wooden bars, and hay spread in mangers before them. The milker sat on a single-legged stool beside the cow, seized a teat in each hand, encircling the base between thumb and first finger, then tightened his fingers, running them from top to bottom of the teat. This yielded a stream of white milk into a galvanized pail held between the knees. Each cow produced one or two gallons of milk in fifteen minutes of milking. The process was not without hazards, as the udder is

The big Muphy Meadow, the first property of Dennis Murphy, where William toiled in his early years.

located so close to the hooves of the cow. Undoubtedly the future priest received many stout kicks.

At the conclusion of the milking, the foaming buckets were taken to the dairy pantry at the rear of the house. Women took over at that point, straining the milk and pouring it into pans. After twelve hours, cream rose to the top and was skimmed off to be used on the dining table or churned into butter. One can be sure that William's hands, like his brother Denis's, developed great strength from his participation in this ranching chore.

While attending school at St. Joseph's Mission, William was influenced by the life and example set by the oblate fathers. He felt a call to serve. At age sixteen he left the 141 Mile Ranch and entered St. Louis College in New Westminster. In 1885 he entered the Novitiate of Lachine in Montreal and was ordained a priest in Ottawa in 1892 by Monsignor Thomas Duhamel.

While studying at St. Louis College he purchased 296 acres of land at Mile 142, and he later received title to lot 43, G-1, Cariboo district. The legal work was put through by old Dennis Murphy, listed as attorney-in-fact for William. This land was later incorporated into the 141 Mile Ranch of Johnny Murphy. People wondered whether Father Murphy had second thoughts about his perpetual vows for the priesthood or simply went along with his father's schemes to enlarge the cattle ranch.

Oblate records show that he was of a quiet and scholarly nature. Following his ordination he entered service as a parish priest at St. Joseph's parish in Ottawa, and he served in this capacity from 1901 to 1915, but his main interest was the academic world. In 1905 he was appointed a teaching fellow and secretary of the University of Ottawa, where he served as dean until 1915. He had an interest in native rights in British Columbia, and Father Coccola mentions that on a trip to Ottawa with native elders, Father Murphy welcomed them and accommodated them in his residence.

The oblate records relate that Father Murphy always had a heart full of concern for others and was a pacifier of racial struggles and unrest in the nation's capital. Father Murphy's obituary reads: "Le pere fut toujours reconnu comme une esprit droit" (The father was always known as a just spirit). He

Some of the Murphys lie at St. Joseph's Mission, only four miles away from Dennis and Ellen's original holdings, but far away from Father Murphy, who is interred in Hull, Quebec.

is now interred at the Cemetery of Notre Dame in Hull, Quebec. Whether he was more of a rancher or a priest or an academic, it might be that his just spirit dwells to this day over his original land grant—section 43, G-1, at the 142 marker on the Cariboo Wagon Road.

CHAPTER 22

AN MP IS BORN

How Philip Mayfield was Prepared for Ottawa

This is a heart-warming tale whose veracity some might question and others disbelieve entirely. Philip Mayfield, MP for Cariboo-Chilcotin, eldest son of Patricia Jeannette, acquired the skills to survive for six years in Ottawa while he was on our Cariboo ranch.

Todd and I were living the full, joyful life of bachelors at Lazy Lee Meadows, finding diversion in feeding 400 head of cattle, cutting water holes, sawing firewood to keep the old Litzenberg house warm in twenty-below weather, and cooking our meals over a wood-burning stove. It was January 1947 when young cousin Philip came into our care. He was used to the soft life of a rancher at the 141 Mile House and pined for the experience of an old-time cattle ranch. He arrived by degrees, coming the eight miles from 141 Mile House to our home ranch, the Hills and Paul, then nine miles further to the Lazy Lee by hay sled over a snowy backwoods trail.

Young as he was, he adjusted quickly, though he wondered why the water buckets brought from the pump into the old Litzenberg house formed a thick layer of ice in no time at all, and why we put on clothes instead of taking them off when we went to bed. He was given the indulgence of Duke, our collie dog, to keep him warm at night.

At our first breakfast Philip asked for corn flakes, reflecting his near-city upbringing.

Philip Mayfield, who also encountered the ice spirit many years ago. He emerged a stronger man.

"Corn flakes? Corn flakes! Real ranchers eat oatmeal porridge."

At dinners he soon acquired an appetite for moose stew, made with onions, tomatoes, and bacon. My brother's sourdough biscuits were eaten without complaint. He was well on his way to becoming a real rancher, what with pumping water from the well, chopping wood, pitching hay, and shovelling cow manure from the barn.

All too soon his three-day holiday came to an end. On Saturday evening, once the cattle were fed and the water holes re-cut, the three of us mounted our horses and prepared to return to the home ranch. There was a cold chill in the air, mist drifted across the meadows, and a few stars shone dimly above. Philip, who had caught a nasty cold in this healthy outdoor environment, coughed miserably and hunched up in his saddle.

Two miles along the way we stopped at Orville Fletcher's winter feeding cabin. After surveying Philip's chilled form in the lantern light, the Fletchers suggested that we leave him behind with them. We looked at him and said, "Oh he's alright. Just sad to be going home." We then started down the snowy trail with six miles to go. At intervals we urged his horse on, but Philip didn't seem to be too talkative. He couldn't stop coughing, and it resonated harshly in the cool night air.

At dusk, while crossing the Two Mile Meadow, we saw two moose browsing in the nearby willows. We were cheered by this sight and shouted to Philip, but he did not seem to share our thrill. He was bent over in his saddle, both hands on the saddle horn, coughing despondently. After two hours, our horses pulled up in front of the ranch house, the thin yellow light from gas lamps shining warmly across the snow and sparks flying out of the chimneys. We could see our mother preparing dinner.

"Okay Philip, we'll let you get off here. We'll feed your horse in the barn."

He didn't answer, so we rode one on each side of him and tried lifting him out of the saddle. For a time we were unsuccessful because the seat of his pants was frozen to the saddle.

To this day, Philip says that all he can remember is getting on the horse at the Lazy Lee and waking up the next morning in his bed at the Hills and Paul Ranch.

A few more days with us and he would have been fitted for a useful life as a cattle rancher. He was denied this golden opportunity by indulgent parents who sent him off to university and, in turn, by the people of the Cariboo who sent him off to Parliament in Ottawa.

Maybe that frozen bottom that he got on his ride from the Lazy Lee will be an advantage in those backbencher seats. He won't be getting any of my moose stew or my brother's sourdough biscuits, though.

In 1996, Philip Mayfield was re-elected to Parliament by the largest majority of any riding in Canada.

CHAPTER 23

APOSTLE OF THE CARIBOO

The Reverend A.D. McKinnon

Alexander Duncan McKinnon was the first resident minister in the Cariboo, arriving at Williams Lake in 1921 and serving the community for the next twenty years. Middle-aged residents of the Cariboo, on checking their baptismal certificates, will likely see his name as officiating clergyman. Some married couples will remember his kindly, genial presence at their nuptials. He was the long-standing minister of Knife Creek Road.

A.D. McKinnon was born in 1866 on the family homestead at East Lake Ainslie, Nova Scotia. He was a Cape Breton Islander and, true to the island's traditions, he came from a family of twelve children. Parents John A. and Catherine McKinnon were Scots, a matter of which Alex was inordinately proud. A picture taken of him as a young man shows him standing before a blackboard on which is written "I am sorry for any one who is not Scotch." There were few who did not fall into this category in the rural community in which he was reared.

His parents were devout Christians and while not wealthy, were strong supporters of higher education. Alex gained a teaching certificate and then obtained a position, earning enough money to send his brothers to university before he himself sought higher education. Two of his brothers became medical doctors and four others became ministers. One remained on the family farm for his entire life.

Alex entered Queen's University in 1890, spending his summer holidays as a student minister out west in the Kootenays of B.C., where he was instrumental in establishing schools at Windermere, Fort Steele, and Galena. In 1896 he was asked to serve in the Cariboo. With all due haste he came west, was ordained a Presbyterian minister at Kamloops, and then journeyed three days by wagon and boat to reach the village of Quesnel. His first official function was to preside over the dedication of a new church.

A story is told of Reverend McKinnon's arrival at Barkerville. After he was introduced to the hotel proprietor as the new preacher, he noticed a sporting event taking place in the street outside the premises. Two large miners were contesting which could throw a rock the farthest. A.D. stepped up and said, "Let me enter your contest." Without taking off his coat, he pitched the stone a full two feet past the previous mark. He was a giant of a man and strong, and thus his reputation was established among the miners as "Big McKinnon."

The Reverend's first marriage ceremony, performed in Fort George for Ernest Sturrock Peters and Betsy Rois, was somewhat of a disaster. The story begins with him having to procure a marriage licence from the government agent in Barkerville. After travelling from Quesnel, he arrived to find that he did not know the name of the bride. The government agent laughed and left a blank space where her name was to be noted, along with a few other blank spaces. All were to be filled in later when ascertained.

The trip to Fort George began under less than auspicious circumstances. His guide felt that the trip was too dangerous and backed out at the last minute. A.D. was not deterred. He crossed the Fraser seated in a riverboat, leaving his horse to swim behind. The horse, with perhaps more sense than A.D., balked, with the whole town watching from the riverbank, and was pushed back into the river by volunteers. A poor swimmer, the beast was submerged three times and nearly drowned. He required hours to dry out.

The trip took four days, and rainy weather plagued both horse and man. An attempt to secure lodging with a native the first night ended with an angry refusal given in the Chinook language, "Klatawa hyack" (go quickly), which A.D. did and spent a miserable night in the open. (It might be noted that the Reverend McKinnon was gifted not only in Gaelic and Greek but also in the local Chinook language.)

On arrival at Fort George he married the happy couple and later baptized their five children. He would have journeyed on to Fort St. James to visit an old friend, Father Coccola, from his Kootenay days, but his horse was not up to the journey. On his return journey to Quesnel he found himself arguing with a bear for a choice sleeping spot under the roots of an overturned tree. A.D. apparently won.

After a year at Quesnel, he wouldn't see the Cariboo again for 24 years. He was called to minister to a large church in Boston, U.S.A.. At one time he was honoured as the most eloquent and popular platform speaker in the city of Boston. His recitations of the works of Robbie Burns were also in great demand. The Scots were much cheered when he preached an entire sermon in Gaelic about once a month. While in Boston, he married Edna Tucker.

Reverend A.D. McKinnon (upper left) and his congregation from the Williams Lake church.

In 1912 he accepted a call to St. Stephen's Presbyterian Church in Vancouver, B.C., and remained there for nine years. During this time, two daughters, Lovett and Joy, were born. They were later to become the famous professional skaters known as the McKinnon Sisters.

In 1921 the call to the Cariboo was strong, and he could not resist an invitation to take over the Cariboo Presbytery, which covered an area twice the size of Nova Scotia, with 21 preaching points. The first year he spent in Clinton while a church and manse were constructed in Williams Lake. He then established his residence in the latter community and was to remain there for the next nineteen years, travelling to far-off points. While he had a large touring sedan, the roads were abominable and he was heard to say, "I have spent a night on almost every hill in the Cariboo, either stuck in a mud hole or with the car broken down from bouncing on the stony roads."

Mrs. McKinnon, who was somewhat younger, often chauffeured the Reverend on his out-of-town trips. He would sit in the rear seat contemplating nature. Whenever they met a fellow traveller he would cry out "Whoa." If it was close to lunch, they invited the traveller to share their provision. Houses along the way were visited, greetings given, and if spiritual needs were evident, the Lord's presence was made known.

Of course he could not preach at all 21 points in the same week, but he did try to make a visit to each place once a month. Services were held in schools, community halls, and people's homes. On occasion it was necessary to clean up beer bottles and the general clutter from a dance the previous night. Most of his congregations were of fifteen people or less. Sometimes only one or two showed up. This did not faze him and he tailored his service to the occasion.

During some summer seasons he was allotted a student minister to help with the work. One of these was Stewart Crysdale, who came in 1940 and was to take over the charge in 1943. Reverend Crysdale, now retired in Toronto, had some amusing anecdotes relating to the Reverend, now Dr. McKinnon after receiving an honorary degree, likely bestowed at Pine Hill, Nova Scotia.

On one occasion, before church could be assembled he took a stout branch and chased a bear away from the school hall at Forest Grove. On another occasion, while preaching at Lac la Hache, a noisy, inebriated individual at the back of the hall interrupted the service. Dr. McKinnon admonished the man on several occasions and finally marched down and seized him by the collar, opened the door, and ejected him into the night. His congregation was impressed. Their minister had not missed a word of his sermon during the whole event.

I remember the marriage of my aunt, Patricia Herber, to Melvin Mayfield of the 141 Mile House. It was a cold November day, and the roads were extremely icy, which made transportation difficult. Dr. McKinnon and his wife and daughters came from Williams Lake, and after the marriage ceremony in the 141 Mile House living room, a festive dinner was served in the parlour. During the dinner a genial A.D. gave a toast to the bride, comparing my Aunt Pat to the fairest rose in the garden. As far as I was concerned, she was more like an Indian paintbrush or a tiger lily out in the forest than a garden flower.

After the wedding, daughters Joy and Lovett practised their skating routines on the ice of the horse-watering pond in front of the barn. They did spins and figures in their sparkling costumes before an appreciative wedding party.

In later years Dr. and Mrs. McKinnon served the Cariboo faithfully, but with failing health. Mrs. McKinnon was no longer able to drive the large touring sedan over the miles of gravel road, and her husband sometimes found his powers too weakened to conduct services. The village knew that if the church bell had not been rung by ten o'clock, there would be no service at eleven. In 1939 Edna passed away, leaving him alone in the manse. Over the next two years he often carried his lunch to her grave at noon, eating his lunch there and spending the hour at the gravesite.

Twenty years of service to the Cariboo passed all too quickly. After the usual retirement age, Dr. McKinnon still carried on, answering a call as pastor to the United Church in Peachland, where he served for five more years.

*The famed McKinnon twins delighted the world
and the Cariboo with their ice-skating talent.*

He was respected by the thousands of people who will never forget his powers as a friend and pastor. Death came peacefully in his 83rd year at the old family homestead, East Lake Ainslie, where he had retired a year previously.

One can imagine A.D. and Edna in the kingdom of heaven, Edna driving the golden carriage, A.D. sitting in the back, taking in the sights and thinking, "This is grand, much like the Cariboo," while in the distance waited their Lord, ready to clasp them to his heart.

CHAPTER 24

HERALDING DR. HERALD

Pioneer Doctor of the Gold-Rush Trail

M edical skills were not highly developed in the Cariboo at the turn of the century, and mothers were often the supreme authority. R. Wilson Herald, a suave, handsome, 1890 graduate of Queen's University, seemed an unlikely candidate to become the medical institution of the gold-rush trail
of central British Columbia.
Even today, as has been the
case since the gold rush,
there is but one main two-
lane, north-south road that
links the Cariboo to the
outside world. This was the
road that he took in 1896,
arriving by a four-horse
stagecoach at the small
community of 150 Mile House.
This was 300 miles north of
Vancouver, 150 miles from
Lillooet on the Royal En-
gineers' Cariboo Wagon Road.

At the turn of the cen-
tury there were no more
than 200 inhabitants at 150

*The handsome R.
Wilson Herald.*

Mile House, scattered in homes along the Cariboo Wagon Road. A rail fence on either side of the roadway kept wandering horses and cows out of the gardens and yards. Along the road came wagons, democrat buggies, and saddle horses heading north toward the gold. Four-horse teams dragged dusty, heavily laden dead x wagons (named for the horizontal x-shaped reinforcement of the wagon frame on either side of the reach) over tortuous roads to Quesnel and Barkerville. From 150 Mile House a road went west to the Onward Ranch, the Fraser River, Chilcotin, and the Pacific Ocean 300 miles away. Another road led east to Harper's Camp, Likely, and Quesnelle Forks. From there a trail led over Yank Mountain to Barkerville.

Dr. Hugh Watt, an 1880 graduate of Toronto, had served the 150 Mile House community for fifteen months on a locum tenens basis, but Dr. Herald was the first full-time medical practitioner there. He was of medium build, fair complexion, and had a full moustache that set off handsome features and a trim athletic physique. He was registered with the British Columbia College of Physicians and Surgeons in 1891, practising the speciality of ear, nose, and throat medicine in Vancouver and the Lower Mainland, then for a year in Ashcroft in central British Columbia. It would seem that his family did not accompany him.

In Queen's graduating class of 1890, Dr. Herald can be found in the bottom row, third from right.

He was thus an experienced practitioner when he set up office in 150 Mile House. Local people were seen in his office or at home, but a rented team and buggy were used for distant house calls, which sometimes meant travel up to 40 miles. At the turn of the century there were less than a dozen medicines effective by modern standards. These were morphine and opium for pain, digitalis for heart failure, bromides as a sleeping potion, ether and chloroform as anaesthetics, and iodine and carbolic acid as antiseptic agents. Aspirin, a very useful drug in today's medicine, was known but not widely used. For serious infections there were no antibiotics. Most basic, common surgical instruments were available. These included pearl-handled scalpels, haemostats, retractors, bone saws, and improvised splints. Some practitioners had obstetrical forceps made for difficult cases. The nearest hospital was in the gold-mining town of Barkerville 100 miles away, and serious illnesses often led to fatal outcomes.

Laura Moore, an early Cariboo pioneer, tells of an emergency appendectomy performed by Dr. Herald on her father. Dr. Herald was notified of John Moore's illness and travelled the twenty miles from 150 Mile House to their Alkali Lake ranch by howler (a two-wheel cart with ungreased wooden axles.) On arrival, Dr. Herald confirmed the diagnosis and operated on a table in the Moore's ranch house, with Mrs. Moore pouring open-drop ether. Following the operation, the doctor remained with the family for several days until recovery was assured.

There's an amusing anecdote attributed to Dr. Herald. It seems a Mrs. Flett of nearby Deep Creek Ranch, a maid working for the Murphy family, was grossly overweight. Diet and exercise having failed, the doctor put her on the second floor of the store at 150 Mile House and locked her in with a small portion of food to last each day. Weeks went by without a pound of weight being lost. One evening, the suspicious medical practitioner quietly walked around the building. He found his patient lustily hauling a pail of food from the ground to her second-storey window with a cowboy's rope tied to the bucket. Her husband was the co-conspirator. The treatment was ended forthwith, and obesity stymies doctors to this day.

150 Mile House, where Dr. Herald first set up practise.

Life at the 150 Mile House was never dull for this dashing young doctor. He was a bachelor, and there were dinners, lively parties, and card-playing evenings. The whole community for miles around joined in the nights of dancing. These went on all night until breakfast at dawn.

In 1901, Dr. Mostyn Hoops, a Master's graduate of the famous Rotunda Hospital in Dublin, came to be Dr. Herald's assistant. Dr. Herald then took a three-year leave of absence from the British Columbia College registry while he joined his brother, only to reappear in 1906 in Cloverdale near Vancouver. In 1914 he moved to Vancouver.

In 1916 he enlisted in the Seaforth Highlanders and was decorated for bravery at the Vimy Ridge battle. In post-war years he organized the Vimy Ridge memorial celebrations in Vancouver. He established a consulting practice specializing in ear, nose, and throat diseases at an office in Nelson, B.C. His practice covered the Okanagan and Kootenay areas.

In 1928, while attending a peripheral consulting clinic in Fernie, B.C., he developed pneumonia and was dead within 24 hours, at only 51 years of age.

Gold and adventure led this son of the manse to the frontier, to war, and to being a medical practitioner in isolated areas. He acquitted himself with distinction in every endeavour.

CHAPTER 25

BULLS AND BANKS

George Mayfield's Mark on the Cariboo

The Mayfields came early to North America, probably prior to the revolutionary war between the United States and Britain. Certainly some animosity lingered on in them, and they always told anyone who cared to listen that they were Scots and not damned Englishmen. George's father, William Garret Mayfield, was a piper in the Union Army during the Civil War between the States and was discharged in 1866 in Arkansas. In 1885 he made his way west along the famous Oregon Trail and settled in central Oregon. There he established a large cattle ranch.

The eldest son of William and Minerva Jane Mayfield was George, born on a cattle ranch near Medford, Oregon. Two other boys followed, Howard and Frank. All three experienced the hardships of growing up on an isolated cattle ranch.

The Mayfields were huge men, and strong. The story is told of George's father finding a bear chasing his pigs. He killed it with his bare hands. George told of going on cattle drives with enough food for two days and being gone for a week on limited rations. On another occasion he was stranded in a deserted cabin that provided shelter but no grass for his horse. He searched the cabin and found some flour, which he mixed with water and cooked as bannock for himself and his horse. Another time he was stranded on an isolated homestead, and the remnants of a garden produced a bumper crop of tomatoes.

For several days all he had to eat was tomatoes, and he would never touch one again throughout his lifetime.

In Oregon, George finished high school and acquired several ranches of his own, one of which he traded for a bank. As president of the bank, he loaned out a considerable amount of money to a rancher, only to find it was an imprudent move. Rather than allowing the bank to take the loss, George paid the mortgage off himself and was in dire financial straits for several years.

Still he prospered, and in 1914 he married Elna F. Schultz, a secretary. Three sons were born to this union: Melvin, Marvin, and Roland. Melvin is the father of Philip Mayfield, member of Parliament for Cariboo-Chilcotin (see chapter 22).

George prospered, not in cattle ranching, but in raising potatoes in Klamath Falls, Oregon. From the sale of this ranch he had the finances to go back into cattle ranching, and his dream was to establish a cattle ranch in British Columbia. In 1935, with his three sons, he bought the 141 Mile House for $35,000 from Angus McLaughlan.

The 141 Mile Ranch had some limitation on hay supply, and when the herd was increased to 600 head of cattle, hay was always a problem. Modern methods of ranching were introduced, and tractors were used on the ranch. Usually there were six cowboys hired to attend to the ranch work and manage the cattle that ranged east of the Cariboo Highway.

In 1939 George and his brother Frank bought the Chilko Ranch, the third largest ranch in British Columbia, running about 2500 head of cattle. Frank's business methods were not congenial to George's way of doing business, and in addition, Frank's wife Margaret was a hellion and kept the ranch in turmoil, so the family moved back to the 141 Mile House and continued the operation there. The overhead on the ranch was high, and finances became precarious. Elna Mayfield was a difficult woman to live with as well, adding to George's burden.

The PGE Railway built the first stockyards in Williams Lake as a shipping point. During the 1930s, cattle shipped to Vancouver often did not bring enough return to pay the freight bill. The two major cattle buyers, Burns and Swift, did not permit any real competition in purchasing deals.

George Mayfield knew that there had to be a better way of marketing the cattle and was instrumental in the founding of the Cariboo Cattlemen's Association. This was a marketing agency that had a field man who would take the buyers to a ranch where they could inspect the cattle and arrive at a fair price. Later, secret bids were given to the field man, and if the rancher didn't like the price, he didn't have to sell but could open the gates and turn the beef back to pasture. On one occasion the Cariboo Cattlemen's Association had an auction sale at Williams Lake. The auctioneer didn't show up, so George Mayfield did the auctioning, with Henry Zirnhelt of the 150 Mile House catching the bids for him. Another time, the buyers refused to pay the going price and all the cattle were on the road to be sold at Williams Lake. George went out to the Chilcotin and bought all of them at a fair price, rented a pasture at Anaheim Reserve for 3000 head, and also rented a pasture at Sugar Cane. He had a corner on the market because he had bought all the other cattle offered. In the end, after he had pastured for six weeks, he sold them for a penny a pound more than he paid.

By 1945 most of the cattle in the Cariboo were sold through the Cattlemen's Association, which was by then securely founded. The association later established a warehouse where supplies for ranchers, including grains, salt, feed pellets and fertilizer, were sold for wholesale prices.

During his time on the 141 Mile House ranch, George noted that the cattle on the range were a varied colour mixture and often rangy and poorly built. The bulls were often scrub bulls that had similar characteristics. In co-operation with Lord Martin Cecil of 100 Mile House, the Cariboo Cattlemen's Association established strict standards for bulls running free on the range. They had powers of enforcement, and soon all the scrub bulls were gone. One aggressive little black bull could not be corralled, and it was shot when one of the 141 Mile House cowboys encountered it out on the range.

At one point George Mayfield almost had a political life. He was asked to accept nomination as a candidate for a major B.C. political party. He seemed ideally suited until the matter of party solidarity was explained to him. He exclaimed, "Does that mean that I would have to vote for something that I was opposed to, just to keep harmony in the party?" He was assured that this was true but that the issue rarely presented itself.

George drew himself up to his full six feet and firmly stated, "That, gentlemen, is something I would never do. Good day." And he walked out.

George was never afraid to stand up for what he felt was right. This resulted in his being shot in a land dispute in Oregon, and he had a bullet hole in his left thigh until the day he died. As a judge at stampedes, he sometimes received the brunt of disagreements as tensions often ran high. On one occasion a disgruntled contestant challenged him to fight on the main street of Williams Lake. George's sons could have beaten the man to a pulp, but they all held back. Although George was 50 years old, the code of the West dictated that he handle the matter himself. He gave as good as he received, but did have a bright bruise on his cheek and a black eye before the affair was ended by mutual agreement.

George became secretary to the Cattlemen's Association in 1945. By this time the three boys were established on ranches of their own, and the 141 Mile House was sold to Fred Hinsche.

It was a matter of great pride and satisfaction for George to be driven out on the range and see the fine Hereford cattle grazing on the open grassy slopes. Each Thanksgiving the Cariboo Cattlemen had an annual bull sale, which was one of the largest in B.C. Up to 150 bulls were sold in a single day. One of George's most pleasurable moments before he died was when he was taken to the bull sales ring in his car and bought a bull at auction. He subsequently gave the bull to his youngest son, Roland.

George's health deteriorated, largely the result of smoking for over 50 years. Emphysema weakened his lungs, and chronic pneumonia brought an early end at just over 70 years of age.

George Mayfield was a prince among men, a man who stood head and shoulders above others in his integrity and loyalty to the code of the Old West. His word was his bond and was surer than any document sworn before a covey of judges. He was fair and honest in all of his dealings, and through his vision he established excellence in the cattle herds of the Cariboo.

George Mayfield.
Almost a politician.

So passed from us a great man. As Shakespeare has Mark Antony say of Brutus in *Julius Caesar*. "His life was gentle; and the elements so mixed in him that nature might stand up and say to all the world, 'This was a man'."

CHAPTER 26

MOUNTAIN OYSTERS TO MOTOR HOMES

Patricia Jeannette, a Real Pioneer Woman

In 1839, Henry Herber left Darmstadt, Kassel Hesse, Germany, for the New World. Maria Krammer, from the same general area in Germany, arrived with him in New York. The two were married, and in three generations, Patricia Jeannette Herber arrived at Fetters Springs, California.

Fetters Springs was in northern California, close to the gold-rush country, in a noted wine-producing area. The Herbers found no gold nuggets at Fetters Springs, and as they believed strongly in temperance, the wine industry had little effect on them. Perhaps it was the roving spirit in these early immigrants from Germany that created the restless urge to move on. The entire family, together with two grandchildren, moved to the Cariboo country of British Columbia in June of 1929. Patricia at this time was ten years old and would be eleven on Christmas Day.

In large families, the eldest daughter traditionally helped her mother with the younger children, and succeeding daughters helped with the cooking and housework. Patricia, eighteen years younger than the eldest daughter, was allowed a good deal more freedom to ride her horse, fish, hunt, milk cows, pitch hay, and generally become involved in ranch activities outside the home. There was only one activity that Patricia refused to participate in. It was tradition at the time of castration of the bull calves to have a barbecue of "mountain oysters." Pat would not partake of this annual delicacy.

School was never a high priority for Patricia Jeannette, yet she struggled on pluckily, being taught at home. Her first boyfriend was young Tommy Whelan, a charming, red-haired, likeable Irish lad. Tommy was slightly older than Patricia, fond of sailing and, in addition, the son of the owner of a large hotel in Vancouver. He and his friend Billy Dale were house-sitting our neighbour's holdings about a mile and a half away. Billy Dale was having wife problems in Vancouver and felt it wise to remove himself from that neighbourhood while things simmered down. Tommy was exuberant, unmarried, and completely fitted to the enjoyment of life as a young bachelor until he met the high-spirited ranch girl.

There were some major impediments to any deepening of their relationship. Tommy was considered too old for Pat because he was six years older. Also, Tommy was a nominal Roman Catholic, and Pat's family had migrated from the Roman Catholic church to the Methodist church and were not inclined to retrace their steps or have one of their children do so. It was also a problem that Tommy's father was rumoured to sell intoxicating beverages in his hotel, including beer. The Herber family abstained from alcohol, and the devil himself would have been more welcome in the home than anyone connected to that specific trade. On one occasion when Tommy appeared with the suspicion of alcohol on his breath, he was not allowed inside for three hours until the hateful vapours had disappeared.

The end of that summer brought tearful good-byes, and shortly afterward Patricia was persuaded to write a "Dear Tommy" letter, and that was the end of it. Or was it? First loves always hold a corner of one's heart, and I suspect that until the end, Patricia kept a space for an exuberant Irishman with flaming red hair.

Over the next year, two things happened in Patricia's life. The first was that she was given a horse of her own, a feisty, dappled, medium-sized mare called Trixie, who in some respects was as set in her ways and as independent-minded as Patricia herself. The second was that the neighbouring ranch,

141 Mile House, was purchased by an American family that had a son called Melvin. Common sense won out over romantic fantasies, and in three month's time, Patricia was engaged to be married to Melvin Mayfield, the most eligible young man in the area.

I remember their wedding day well. It was November, the weather was cold, and the roads were so slippery that it was impossible to make the eight-mile trip to the 141 Mile Ranch by any means other than walking. The wedding was held in the Mayfields' ranch house, and an elaborate dinner followed.

Getting along with the in-laws proved a trial to Melvin and Patricia in their new married life. Since Melvin was away from home most of the day, it was not as hard for him as it was for Patricia, who lived immediately across the road from her in-laws. Her mother-in-law was as headstrong as Patricia, and the sparks flew. The situation eased somewhat in the first winter when Melvin and Pat moved the cattle back to the Halfway Ranch, eighteen miles to the east of the main road.

On a cold January day, Patricia set forth to follow her husband and the cattle on the narrow road on which the argonauts had arrived eight years earlier. At the top of a long hill coming out of the Murphy Meadow, Patricia dismounted from Trixie to slide the bar latching the gate. As she leaned over to slide the wooden bar back, Trixie, in somewhat of a pique, bit the chilled Pat on the derrière. Both females were cold and somewhat touchy. Pat took the locking bar out of the gate and whacked Trixie across the flank while Trixie attempted to bite and kick.

They finally completed the next two miles, bringing Pat into the warmth of our home for a short time, while Trixie enjoyed a warm barn. Patricia had layers of newspaper underneath her outer clothing for insulation. When she had warmed up and had a bite to eat, they set out again in the early darkness of four o'clock. When one is young and in love, ten miles on a wintry day is probably not too long.

Melvin and Pat's first winter was spent in an idyllic setting in a two-room log cabin home with 300 hungry cattle to be fed. It was in this setting that young Philip was conceived, and he arrived the following fall.

Donald followed in about a year's time, amidst a flurry of excitement trying to get his mother to the hospital in time. When Patricia had her first contractions, we were all stuck in the family car, entrenched in mud thirteen miles back of the main road. Aunt Alice seemed to know something about this and assured everyone that all would be well and that Donald

The wedding of Patricia Herber and Melvin Mayfield at the 141 Mile House on November 26, 1936, Dr. McKinnon officiating. From left: Jack Lapinski, Grandma Schulz, Mrs. McKinnon, Dr. McKinnon, Ethelyn Herber, George Mayfield, Melvin Mayfield, Patricia Mayfield, Johnny Dodd, Joyce Snider Mayfield, Doug Mallet, Shirley Lee Ennest, Archie Herber, Harry Barnard, and Stanley Herber. Eldon and Todd Lee are in front.

would indeed be born in the hospital at Williams Lake, 33 miles away, rather than in the back seat of the car. Thankfully, she was right.

Then the war years came, and Patricia's one desire was to be part of the fight. She would have given her eyeteeth to be an ambulance driver as close to the front as possible. But while Melvin was a captain in the home reserves, there was little opportunity for military service, their position being judged more important on the ranch and in the raising of their family.

After the war, Melvin and Patricia moved from 141 to the Alkali Lake Ranch, where Melvin was field boss for Baron Von Riedemann. Following two years of this, they bought their own ranch at last, the Springhouse Ranch. More children followed: a third boy Gordon, then Ann, their one girl, and last was Roy, all born while they were living at their ranch.

Life for a pioneer wife was difficult, and work was from sunrise to sundown and often into the late hours of the night. The family lived in a three-room log house, with small log buildings in proximity that housed the older children. The cooking was done over a woodstove that had to be nursed into life in the morning and put to bed late at night. Washing was done with a rather primitive machine in a separate building, and because there were five children, long lines of clothing were strung on the outside lines. The boys from early on were educated, first in the small country school near Springhouse, and later on in Williams Lake, which necessitated a twenty-mile bus trip every morning and night.

One of the main meadows of the Springhouse Ranch was seventeen miles east by wagon road, and this required Melvin to be away for a good part of the winter in a remote cabin to feed the cattle. Patricia then had the added responsibilities of supervising the ranch chores and feeding the milk cows, pigs, and chickens.

Patricia, if a little naïve, had a natural engaging friendliness. She thought nothing of opening a conversation with a total stranger to exchange opinions and views and past histories. This occasionally let her into some amusing predicaments. Once, when she was with the Lee family on a holiday at Prince Rupert, the group desired a boat trip across the harbour and was looking for a charter craft. Patricia left the group and then bounded back, full of enthusiasm. Behind her stumbled a disgruntled First Nations representative.

"Guess what," she said. "This man will take us all over the harbour in his own boat and it won't cost us a cent. All we have to do is wait until he gets a few leaks in the boat stopped up and we're on our way."

I looked over our proposed captain and was not impressed. He was about 50 years old, unshaven, somewhat smelly, and dressed in grease-stained, rough clothing. He also smelled to high heaven of beer and looked like he had been on a weeklong drinking spree.

"No worry," he said. "I take you and it won't cost you a cent. Just need to plug a few leaks and we're on our way. Could you loan me ten dollars while I get some pitch to stop the leaks in the boat, and then we're on our way."

Somewhat dubiously I loaned him the money, and that was the last we saw of our captain. We ended up catching the scheduled charter boat out through the harbour and into the Pacific Ocean, where we were turned back by rolling waves which made everyone seasick except Pat. She seemed caught up in what had happened to the captain.

Ranching entails much work and hardship, and there are also tragedies. If one looks carefully, small graveyards can be found on most of the older ranches of the Cariboo. When their daughter, Ann, was four years of age, she contracted scarlet fever and was given one of the early wonder drugs, Sulfa. She developed an overwhelming allergic response to the drug and died despite all available medical care. Melvin and Patricia never completely recovered from this tragedy, and for years the silent agony strained the bonds of their marriage. Young people are able to cope somewhat better, and the boys one by one completed their high-school education and grew into responsible young men with endurance, responsibility, and conscientiousness imparted by the ranch life and their extended families.

Melvin and Patricia continued to ranch. They had a modest degree of success because Melvin—who was a good rancher, conscientious and thorough in all his undertakings—practised good farming methods, even going so far as to heat the water that the cattle drank in the winter. At this time, however, ranching was fading as an occupation in the Cariboo district. Logging and lumbering were the prominent industries, and the Springhouse Ranch was sold to another American family, the Lindes. Melvin and Pat moved to Williams Lake, and with their family established a trucking firm. This prospered, and after many years of hard physical labour, the time came for their retirement. The boys had established their own careers. Philip had graduated from UBC and Philip's Academy in the east and took up the United Church ministry. Donald went through several vocations, including ranching and long-distance truck driving, and finally became a machinist in Gibraltar Mines. Gordon continued in the lumber industry for a time, then got into farm machinery sales, and finally became a maintenance foreman with the school district. Roy completed his engineering degree at the University of British Columbia and now has an engineering firm in Seattle. All of them got married and established their own homes.

Unfortunately, Melvin's retirement lasted only a few months. He was lost in a tragic accident while fishing. Patricia got lonely. She was used to being in the thick of activities and having fun and adventure. Serving meals on wheels, singing in the choir, golfing, and visiting others did not quite fill the void left with the loss of her husband.

Then came John. He had lost his wife a number of years before, and he had been lonely as well. There was one obstacle. John lived in Alberta, and Patricia lived in central British Columbia, but a friendship developed over the phone. One day they decided to meet at the junction of Highway 97 and Timothy Lake Road, just outside of a Mayfield family reunion, John in his motor home and Pat in her little Plymouth Reliant. Their budding relationship was the outstanding topic amongst the family. John fit right in, and it was as if we had known him as long as anyone else there. He and Patricia seemed to have a common bond, and we watched their relationship develop quickly. By the fifth day of the family reunion, John and Patricia had decided that they were going to be married.

Like a young girl who is deeply in love but determined to be happy, Patricia's message to one of her children was cryptic and to the point. "I am being married at twelve o'clock two days from now and hope you will come. Bye-bye, Pat." John, I think, gave a somewhat similar message to his children, and plans proceeded in spite of the horrified responses of their children, who thought that they were moving much too quickly. Despite their disapproval, the marriage took place.

The next evening, Patricia picked up her blankets and pillows from my mother's cottage and marched over and plunked them into John's motor home, and two days later they were on their way back to Alberta. After four and a half years, during which time they visited the Northwest Territories, went on many fishing expeditions, travelled, made friends, visited John's son Danny on his nearby farm—in short, doing all the things that they had wanted to do in their years of lonely single life, the last great adventure came.

Shortly before Christmas, Patricia was ice fishing and felt ill. Investigations revealed advanced cancer. The end came quickly, and who can say that this is not the best end: to be free of pain, surrounded by friends and loved ones, a loving husband close by, and the hope of heaven before her.

Patricia Jeannette Herber Mayfield Boldt, the pioneer, wife, mother, and friend of many, may have been one of the giants commemorated on stone, but if you seek living testimony of her giant status, take a look around.

Pat in 1987 with Philip, Donald,
Gordon, and Roy: living testimonies.

CHAPTER 27

MONUMENTS OF JUSTICE

Denis Murphy's Rise to Greatness

Mr. Justice Denis Murphy, when he paid tribute to his and my ancestors and all of the pioneers that built the Cariboo, immortalized them by his words "They were giants in those days." My giants, those pioneer titans of my youth, resided along Knife Creek Road. In stature, few of them exceeded the norm, but in heart and spirit they knew few equals. Denis Murphy was just as much a giant of the Cariboo as any that he was commemorating.

Born in the family's framed log house beside the Cariboo Highway, Denis was not always learned and powerful. Old Annie Basil told my mother, Shirley Lee, of Ellen Murphy's premature labour. Denis, at birth, was puny and weak.

As Annie told the story, she had twisted her hands and made a wry face. "When I am there, the little babies don't die, they live." The pioneer wives possessed considerable medical knowledge, and the skill and common sense of the mother was often the difference between life and death for her children. Long before the discovery of alimentary hydration for vomiting and diarrhea, mothers saved the lives of dehydrated children by dropping small amounts of chicken broth into their mouths over many hours. They stitched gaping cuts with black thread, and even weathered appendicitis by positioning the child in the semi-recumbent position. With serious infections, critical illnesses, or severe injuries, the stricken ones often did die. Most large families lost one or two children, and tiny graves were mute testimony to these tragedies. At such times it was only the support and comfort of friends and neighbours that sustained the bereaved family in its grief. Luckily, Denis, a tiny baby born in an upstairs rancher bedroom, did live and thrive.

Denis was the one "n" Murphy. His father was Dennis. He was a bookish lad, but this did not shield him from the tedious round of chores on the 141 Mile Ranch. He fetched wood for the kitchen stove and brought yard-long blocks of wood for the great heating stove in the living room. At day's end he gathered enough eggs from the chicken run behind the house to supply the family dining table and the tables of the hired men and paying guests, who ate their meals in a separate room off the kitchen. He milked cows and learned to make cream and other dairy products for the ranch and the market. Ellen Murphy was renowned for her dairy butter.

Denis learned something of the rougher side of life at an early age. To reach his bedroom upstairs, he passed the front parlour where his father tended the bar. Old Dennis was a quick-tempered shanty Irishman, and any disagreement was an occasion for confrontation. A million Irish had perished under the British by starvation, and Dennis made it clear that one more stiff wouldn't matter much.

Years later, in the midst of an election debate, a political opponent suggested that Denis was not knowledgeable enough about farming to represent a rural riding. Denis promptly issued a challenge to milk as many cows as his adversary wished. His challenge was not accepted.

His formal education was started as a resident at St. Joseph's Mission under the oblate fathers and nuns. At age sixteen, urged on by his parents, he journeyed east to Ottawa University. Six years later Ellen and Dennis sat in the great assembly hall of Ottawa University and listened to their son give the valedictory address. They nearly burst with pride as he was awarded practically every academic medal. His final PhD thesis was defended in a 45-minute address given entirely in Latin before his faculty mentors.

His brothers, William and James, and his sister, Mary, attended Ottawa University with him. It speaks much to their parents' reverence for education that they financed the university degrees of four children at such a distance from the ranch. It was impossible to bring them home in the summer, so their stay at the university was for the entire time of their academic involvement.

Denis undertook another three years' study at the University of Victoria, where he completed requirements for a law degree and entered practice in Vancouver. It was during this time that his wife of one year died of tuberculosis, a disease that was the scourge of the New World Irish. As a successful lawyer in Ashcroft, Denis was first elected as an MP for Victoria. He then married Maude Cameron of Cornwall, Ontario. She was his brother John's sister-in-law and a friend from university days.

In 1909 he surrendered his practice in Ashcroft when called to the B.C. Supreme Court, a position he was to fill with honour and dignity for the next 32 years. His legal decisions were buttressed with such intense research and profound wisdom that they were seldom upset. He was a strong upholder of courtroom decorum and tradition, firmly believing that the rule of law was the surest guarantee of democracy.

Remembering the days when a university education was hard to achieve because children were separated from their home and family for so long, and because the university experience had benefited him so much, he became a strong supporter of the University of British Columbia. He believed in academic freedom, the right to search unimpeded and unhampered for truth and the right to express that truth freely. This is an issue still under debate today.

Justice Murphy was appointed to the Board of Governors of the University of British Columbia in 1917 and served there until 1941. His daughter, Sally, was likewise honoured and was thrilled to serve on the board beside her father.

Denis was the proud father of five children. William Cameron was a brigadier in World War II, his daughter Sally became a professor of English at UBC, the twins Denis and Paul became lawyers, and the second daughter, Margaret, became a respected wife and mother living in Washington, D.C.

Death came in 1947 to this brilliant student, wise jurist, orator, historian, husband, and father. He had sprung from the Cariboo land on the banks of Knife Creek Road and achieved greatness. In the Latin of his university discourses, "nullum quod tetigit non ornavit" (There was nothing which he touched that he did not adorn).

SPEECH BY THE HON. DENIS MURPHY AT UNVEILING OF MONUMENT AT YALE, JUNE 27, 1925.

... "They met the sun's bravado
And saw below them fold on fold,
Grey to pearl and pearl to gold,
Cariboo like a land of old,
The land of Eldorado."

There they found it, the golden treasure of their long quest, in such quantities that the news of the discovery soon ringed the earth. And with this news came an insistent demand for quicker and better means of transportation ... Almost from where we stand can be heard the crash of falling trees and the reverberations of mighty blasts, for men are busy rebuilding the old road. Soon once again will it stretch in a long white ribbon from Yale to Cariboo. But for us who would have the old-time remembrance it will not be the Cariboo Road. Fallen from its high estate it will be but one link in a tourist road stretching in the not-distant future across the continent. And so we are gathered here to-day to dedicate this monument of enduring granite to the memory of the old road and to the memory of the men of strong hands and stout hearts that built it, for had they not raised the stone we had not found the jewel. We would confer on them such immortality as we can. So long as stand this massive cairn so long will passers-by inquire its purpose. The old story when told in reply must needs provoke a look of wonder, almost of awe, at the frowning canyon yonder and compel the tribute:—

"They were giants in those days."

Yes, indeed, they were giants in those days. God grant that we who reap in comfort where they sowed in hardship may in our daily tasks quit ourselves as men worthy of such sires.

Portions of the speech made by Hon. Denis Murphy.

CONCLUSION

Oh, little Knife Creek, though you are low among the streams and rivers and though your road was dusty in summer, snowbound in winter, and muddy and rutted in all other seasons, still you were the rich soil from which sprang famous men and women, and from along your way many significant events came into being.

Who could imagine that from your banks would arise four ministers of the Lord, ranchers, lawyers, a supreme court judge, medical doctors, members of Parliament, war heroes, and progressive ranchers? Heroic women nurtured their families and carried the burden of backbreaking daily toil while bearing healthy children and raising them with a clear sense of right and wrong and a commitment to the welfare of others through education and service.

The distant past was shaped by the Shuswap people, who arrived from Asia thousands of years ago and had carved out a territory through many conflicts with the fierce Chilcotin Indians to the west of the Fraser River. This people endured and lived from the land but did not change it, a way of life that has not continued.

The present began with the explorers, Alexander Mackenzie and Simon Fraser, and then the fur traders. Then came the gold seekers, who followed the Indian trails to the headwaters of Knife Creek and on to Horsefly. Following the gold seekers were the builders, like Murphy who established Knife Creek Road, and Felker who cut the historic Felker Trail.

The origins of the early pioneers were diverse. All added flavour to this new country, and from their different backgrounds came new wisdom and methods to improve established practices. The argonauts and others from the

United States brought capital and adventurous spirits to the Cariboo and Knife Creek country. All of these people became giants, incorporating the energies, wisdom, and strengths of those who had settled the land.

A tour of the cemeteries in the central Cariboo is a sobering experience. The graves and headstones make one aware of individual mortality, but also give insight into the lives of those who have gone before. But more than anything, it makes one realize that the passing of a generation and a way of life is perfectly natural, that one generation paves the way for another. In the case of the giants of the Cariboo, they did not only clear the land. They opened the way for a new way of life, leaving behind them comfort and ease of a beaten path, conditions that rarely do anyone any good.

Now there is a new breed of argonauts who may not be ranchers or farmers or homesteaders. But they are pioneers. Like Annie, they also are bridges between what came before and what is to come. Annie united the pioneers to the past, where they could see the importance of knowing every yard of the central Cariboo, every stick, every stone, and every tree. We could watch her live off the land and realize that the earth was not hostile, but essentially life-giving.

Let this generation and those to come, in a time of great calamity and change on the earth, challenge whatever lies ahead, the unknown, the dangers, and the new demands of a complex future. May they push against the boundaries imposed by poverty and human strife, challenge the frontiers of time and space, and be worthy of those who have gone before. May they become members in the family of giants.

BIBLIOGRAPHICAL SOURCES
AND ACKNOWLEDGEMENTS

I have not completed a formal bibliographical list, since while the historical facts are valid, in a number of instances they are presented in a romantic vein. Also, a bare bibliographical list does not give an indication of the books' importance to the author.

I would like to list the following sources as especially valuable in establishing the details concerning historical events or persons.

1. On the native Indian legends and geography of Cariboo countryside:

    Symington, Fraser. *The Canadian Indian*. Toronto: McClelland and Stewart, 1969.

    Morice, Father Adrian Gabriel. *The History of the Northern Interior of British Columbia*. Smithers, B.C.: Interior Stationers, 1970.

    Personal communication with the following native people:
    Annie Basil, Sugar Cane Reservation, Interior Salish.
    Donald Sinclair, Kitwanga, Tsimshian Tribal Group.
    Donald Gray, Hagwilget Nation.

2. Chinook as a spoken language comes from contact with local Salish people, Annie Basil, Able Dick, Liza Dick, and Peter Grouse. Excellent resource books are:

    Thomas, Edward Harper. *Chinook, a History and Dictionary*. Portland, Oregon: Binford and Morts, 1970.

    Barnsley, John. *Dictionary of the Chinook Jargon*. Victoria, B.C.: T.N. Hibben & Co.

    Pei, Mario. *The story of Language*. New York, Boston, 1949. (See page 52. This famous book legitimizes Chinook as a recognized form of communication among the world's languages.)

3. On the Irish Murphys, the following sources were especially helpful:

    Cahill, Thomas. *How The Irish Saved Civilization.* Toronto: Doubleday Publishing, 1995.

    Patenaude, Branwen. *Trails to Gold*, vol. 2. Surrey, B.C.: Heritage House Publishing, 1996.

    Archives of British Columbia, Creighton, Sally Murphy. Mr Justice Murphy, U.B.C. Alumni Chronicles. 989.

    Murphy, The Honourable Denis. "The Building of the Cariboo Road." A speech given in Yale B.C. in 1925. BCARS NV 9066862.

    B.C. Department of Land, Titles and Conveyances. Records from 1860 to 1918. Victoria, B.C.

    Vancouver Province, May 2, 1947. "Death Calls Pioneer Judge."

    Personal communication with the following pioneers gave much background information:

    > Emma Felker Bellmond Young (deceased 1949), Duncan, B.C.
    > Shirley Herber Lee Ennest, Mission, B.C.
    > Alice Herber Lindstrom, Stanwood, Washington.
    > Rev. Stanley Herber, San Diego, California.
    > Marie Case Fletcher, 144 Mile House, B.C.

4. Information on Dr. Cheadle and Viscount Milton was obtained from two books:

    Cheadle, Walter B. *Cheadle's Journal of the Trip Across Canada, 1862-1863.* Edmonton: Hurtig Publishers, 1971.

    Milton, Viscount, and Dr. W.B. Cheadle. *The Northwest Passage by Land.* London: Cassell, Petter & Galpin, 1867. This book was in the possession of a descendant of Dr. Cheadle and was printed in 1867.

5. The History of the Argonauts was based on family records compiled in 1965 by Rev. Stanley Herber, one of the original sojourners.

6. The chapters on John Haley, Harry Barnard, Claus Mikkelsen, Orville Fletcher, and Lillian Dodd came from years of contact, as the subjects were near neighbours and were known personally to the author.

7. I am grateful to Donna Sweet of Calgary, Alberta, niece of Gertie Dussault Tressierra, who supplied fascinating

historical information on the Dussault family. The original Dussault came to Quebec seven generations before from a small village in France called Calvin. The legend persists that in France the family was Protestant but converted to the Catholic church in Quebec. The French town, Calvin, is the clue, and the Dussault family was likely Huguenot in France.

8. Alice Isnardy Marchuk provided much historical material in the form of family history, baptismal and marriage certificates, and legal documents on the Isnardy family, which began in 1854 with the immigration of a fourteen-year-old Basque to Mexico. He was later to marry an Indian princess of Lillooet and founded a dynasty that extends to the modern generation, 150 years later. Family members confirm Charlie's habit of talking to his horses. Irene Stangoe's book *Looking Back*, published by Heritage House, also gives information on this fascinating family.

9. Maxine Clark of Knife Creek Road provided much information on the Dodd family. She was a niece, and at the present time her residence property adjoins John's post-war ranch. The pictures were supplied by her, with the original of a copy of General Montgomery and John Dodd coming from the Canadian Army Photography Service of 1944.

10. Information on the quiet priest, William Joseph Murphy, was translated from the French records of the Oblates. Les Oblats au Canada. 1941. The source was Ulric, Robert, O.M.I. Le R.P. Guillaume Murphy, 1865 - 1915, dans Missions ... des ... Oblats de Marie-Immaculée, 62 (1928), pp. 127-132. Records of the Department of Land Titles and Conveyances in Victoria, B.C., were consulted regarding his land acquisitions at 141 Mile House.

11. The Honourable Philip Mayfield is a cousin, and the account of his historic ride from the Lazy Lee Ranch to the Hills and Paul Ranch on Knife Creek Road was printed originally in the *Williams Lake Advocate*, May 6, 1997. Its submission immediately prior to the last

federal election was not entirely without political
motives. Philip won by a landslide in the Cariboo-
Chilcotin riding.

12. On the Reverend A.D. McKinnon, archivist Bob Stewart
and the archives of the United Church of Canada, in
Vancouver, B.C., were most helpful. So too were Dr.
Stewart Crysdale of Toronto and Shirley Ennest, a
former parishioner of Dr. McKinnon, as was I. A final
source was:

Runnalls, F.E., B.A.,B.D. *A History of Prince George.* Fraser
Fort George Museum Society, 1946. (See page 72.)

13. On the pioneer doctor R.T. Wilson Herald, personal
communications from Laura Moxan were helpful. The
anecdote regarding the obese Mrs. Flett was supplied
by Dr. John Roberts, Williams Lake. The Medical
Registers from 1896-1924 supplied by the College of
Physicians and Surgeons gave much useful information
as to appointments and areas of practice.

14. Donald Mayfield of Kamloops gave much information
about the family of the Mayfields. In addition, the
Mayfield ranch adjoined our own and the author was
related by marriage to the Mayfields.

15. Much material was obtained through personal
experiences with the pioneers themselves, who gave
their reminiscences of stories, rumours, and legends
that were common knowledge and freely com-
municated through the ranching settlements. I assume
full responsibility for the accuracy of these.

Oh yes, I must not forget Jane Goodall in regard to
primates and women in estrous:

Goodall, Jane. *The Chimpanzees of Gombe.* Cambridge:
Beltnap Press, 1986.

Eldon Lee
Prince George, B.C., 1999

INDEX

PHOTO CREDITS

BCARS (26 l: A-02361, r: number unknown, 28: number unknown, 34: D-08238, 36: A-03908, 49 l: 60219, r: C-08591), Dolly Petrowitz (48), Irene Stangoe (27, 54, 120, 123), Vancouver Public Library (12).

The remainder of the photos are courtesy of the author.

Denis Murphy's speech (144) BCARS NW 906 B862 [1925].

The sketch of Annie Basil (19) is by Michelle Muntau.

THE AUTHOR

There is no doubt that I have mellowed through the years. In the RCAF I was a self-proclaimed hot pilot nicknamed Buzz. In university I was called "The Brain," and in my years of medicine I tried to be "Super Doc." Now I'm happy to be simply Me, a loving husband to Marjorie, doting father to six and grandfather to eight, author, classics buff, and Sunday School teacher. No more Type A personality for me. I am a committed lay-about. During my life I have formed an indissolvable bond to the rude landscape of the Cariboo. And this bond is more truly recognized because I have had the opportunity for an advanced education. Somehow, I feel that through eternity my spirit will be one with this land, unfettered by the constraints of time and space, a dimension of the Giant standing astride the Deep.

My Hobby

Just to lie and watch the clouds go floating by,
Serene and high.
And if it happens to be raining,
Like any frog I croak complaining
Of bugs and bites and flies and such,
And folks that chatter overmuch.
Of boys with spots and fuzzy down,
Of girls that giggle up and down.
And if there's snow and wind and cloud,
I sit and grumble, "I'll be blowed."
In short, my hobby's like a feather,
It all depends upon the weather.

R.G. Dunbar (Latin teacher, 1939)

And the weather? – Sunny.

* * *

Dr. Lee writes this book from a unique perspective. He was raised on an isolated ranch on Knife Creek Road in the central Cariboo of British Columbia. Here wood was cut for heating, water carried into the house in pails, cows milked for milk and butter, and chicken kept for eggs and meat. He has experience riding for cattle in winter snow, frozen to the saddle, and he suffered the torment of flies and heat while working long summer days on the ranch. Early education was given by his mother and gained by reading thousands of books.

At age nineteen his eyes were opened wide with enlistment in the RCAF, experiencing wartime as a bomber pilot in aircrew. Following this an academic life beckoned, first at Seattle Pacific University, then the University of Washington. He undertook further studies in Canada and England. After thirteen years of academic pursuits he had earned the degrees of Bachelor of Science, Doctor of Medicine, Fellow of Canadian Surgical Society, and Fellow of American Surgical Society. Late in life he received post-graduate credits in Ancient Greek from Regent College at UBC.

He has maintained a bond with the Knife Creek country of his origin. Like Old Annie Basil, he knows "this stick, that stick, this rock, that rock." When he recently pointed out a fir tree to one of the younger generation as the largest tree in the area, the nephew skeptically questioned how he knew. "Simple," was the reply. "I know every tree here."

The author near Squawks Lake.

THE CARBIOO OF DR. LEE ...
PIONEER VOICES AND PEOPLE FROM
HERITAGE HOUSE

They Were Giants in Those Days is the latest offering in the Heritage House collection of Eldon Lee's reminiscences of life in the Cariboo. These books explore the lives and accomplishments of men and women who epitomize the pioneer spirit and resilience that characterize this country. All his books include a blend of personal and archival photos.

Scalpels and Buggywhips—Dr. Lee's tribute to his professional ancestors. For decades Dr. Lee gathered material dating back to early Indian shamans. A long-serving practictioner in his own right, he knew some of his pioneer subjects personally. ($16.95)

Tall in the Saddle—Written with his brother Todd, this book finds two brothers sharing their recollections and observations about growing up on the Hills and Paul Ranch in the Cariboo regions of British Columbia. ($14.95)

A Western Doctor's Odyssey—Like many young men in the 1940s, Dr. Lee faced a calling that would forever change his life. This is the story of those formative years and the unique community where he first practised, a refreshing reminder of what the practice of medicine is all about. ($11.95)